The Battle of Naseby and the Fall of King Charles I

Maurice Ashley

ST. MARTIN'S PRESS · New York

HOUSTON PUBLIC LIBRARY

First published in the United States of America in 1992

All rights reserved. For information, write:
Scholarly and Reference Division,
St. Martin's Press Inc. · 175 Fifth Avenue
New York · NY 10010

ISBN 0-312-07949-4

Library of Congress Cataloging in Publication Data

Ashley, Maurice, 1907–
    The Battle of Naseby and the fall of King Charles I/Maurice
Ashley
        p.   cm.
    Includes bibliographical references and index.
    ISBN 0-312-07949-4
    1. Naseby (England), Battle of, 1645.   2. Charles I, King of
England, 1600–1649.   3. Great Britain—History—Civil War,
1642–1649.   I. Title
    DA415.A76   1992
941.06′2–dc20   91–42966
                                                    CIP

Printed in Great Britain

CONTENTS

LIST OF ILLUSTRATIONS

COLOUR PLATES (*between pp. 80 and 81*)

1 Charles I when Prince of Wales, by Daniel Mytens, 1623 (from a private Scottish collection)
2 Prince Rupert, detail from *Prince Rupert, Colonel William Murray and Colonel John Russell* by William Dobson, *c.* 1644 (National Trust Photographic Library; © National Trust 1991)
3 General Thomas Fairfax by an unknown artist (Cromwell Museum, Huntingdon)
4 *Prince Rupert's Charge at the Battle of Naseby* by Sir John Gilbert RA, 1872 (on loan to Central Museum and Art Gallery, Northampton)
5 The execution of Charles I, by an unknown artist, 1649 (by permission of the Earl of Rosebery)
6 Oliver Cromwell by Robert Walker (Cromwell Museum, Huntingdon)

Black-and-white photographs and illustrations are reproduced by kind permission of the following: Ashmolean Museum, Oxford: 13, 17, 19, 25, 40, 47, 48; The Bodleian Library, Oxford: 11, 54, 61; British Library, London: 31 (with thanks to Sir Charles Rowley and Tozer Marshall Design Associates); British Museum, London: 15; Carisbrooke Castle Museum, Newport, Isle of Wight: 58; Central Museum and Art Gallery, Northampton: 41, 42; The Administrative Trustees of the Chequers Trust: 5; Chester City Record Office: 46; Chester City Record Office and Chester Archaeological Society: 9, 26, 27; The Countess Spencer: 10; Cromwell Museum, Huntingdon: 18, 23, 33, 39 (with acknowledgement to the Royal Armouries HM Tower of London), 44, 52, 55, 59; The Duke of Northumberland: 49 (photo: English Life Publications); The Trustees of Goodwood House: 22; National Army Museum, London: 14; National Library of Scotland, Edinburgh: 4; National Portrait Gallery, London: 1, 3, 6, 7, 8, 12, 20, 24, 30, 36, 37, 38, 50, 56, 62; Scottish National Portrait Gallery, Edinburgh: 16, 28, 51, 57, 63; Somerset Archaeological and Natural History Society: 21, 45. Reproduced by gracious permission of Her Majesty The Queen are illustrations 2 and 53, from the Royal Collection, St James's Palace, London, and illustration 60 from Windsor Castle, Royal Library (© 1991).

INTRODUCTION

The battle of Naseby, fought on the morning of Saturday 14 June 1645, determined the defeat of King Charles I in the first English civil war. A distinguished military historian once wrote that 'no battlefield on English soil apart from Hastings is more famous than Naseby', and that 'never so complete a victory in a major battle on land' had taken place in England 'since the battle of Hastings'.[1]

It is often assumed that because after Charles went north at the beginning of 1642 the Parliamentarians or 'Roundheads', who were at war with the Royalists or 'Cavaliers', commanded the resources of London, the most populous and wealthy city and busiest port in the country, containing the weaponry in the Tower, their ultimate victory was foreordained. Indeed, the Royalist Sir Philip Warwick wrote that 'London' was 'an inexhaustible fountain and such a hydra that if it had one head cut off there sprung up presently another'.[2] Yet, in fact, until the eve of Naseby the Royalists more than held their own throughout the first civil war. Nearly everywhere the Parliamentarian armies experienced setbacks during 1643, when the Royalists were victorious in Cornwall and Devon, gained control of Yorkshire, captured Bristol, the second largest port in the kingdom, and would have succeeded in advancing into the capital had they not been checked by the London trained bands at the first battle of Newbury. The English Parliamentarian leaders were therefore obliged to hire a Scottish army under a professional general to restore their military fortunes, which until then had only prevailed in East Anglia, where Oliver Cromwell was beginning to win his reputation as a cavalry officer.

Even after that, during 1644, although because of the arrival of the Scottish army much of the north of England was lost by the Royalists, King Charles as his own Commander-in-Chief revealed himself to be a tactician of skill and intelligence, winning two victories of note and outmanoeuvring three of the Parliamentarian generals.

From the outset of the war Charles had converted the university city of Oxford into his political capital and military base. The colleges became royal palaces or administrative offices and cloisters were used as arsenals. The town's ramparts rendered it almost impregnable to assault. From Oxford the route that led into Wales, which was mostly Royalist in its support and a source of recruits to the King's army, remained open to the Cavaliers until just before the battle of Naseby so that it could be claimed that Charles commanded inner lines whence he could thrust out in any direction and therefore prevent the Roundheads from dominating the Midlands. It was because Charles had been so far successful in fighting the civil war that Parliament was obliged at the start of the campaign of 1645 to establish what was to be known as the 'New Model Army' under the command of its most able general, Sir Thomas Fairfax. Even then the Committee of Both Kingdoms (England and Scotland), which directed the strategy of the war from London, was perplexed about what was the best course to follow to ensure victory over the King.

Charles, on the other hand, was feeling extremely confident about his prospects when he set out from Oxford on 7 May 1645 with an army of over 11,000 men who were battle-hardened. He had recently heard from James Graham, Marquis of Montrose, who had been fighting gloriously with a tiny force of highlanders in Scotland on his behalf: 'I am in the fairest hopes of reducing this kingdom to your Majesty's obedience,' he wrote, and added, 'I doubt not before the end of the summer I shall be able to come to your Majesty's assistance with a brave army.'[3] Earlier Charles had informed his wife, Queen Henriette Marie, who was in exile in France, that, 'The general face of my affairs is improving,' so that, provided he obtained reasonable supplies of money and powder, he felt certain he would be in a better position when the campaign began than at any time since the rebellion against him broke out.[4] Indeed he still possessed the resources necessary to destroy the New Model Army and win the war; one modern historian expresses the opinion that if Charles and his advisers had behaved 'with the caution and dexterity they had displayed in the summer of 1644 victory or an honourable peace would have been within their reach'.[5] On 9 June 1645, five days before the battle of Naseby, Charles could write to Sir Edward Nicholas, his Secretary of State, resident in Oxford: 'If we peripatetics get no more mischances than you Oxfordians are come to have this summer we may all expect probably a merry winter.'[6] But all his hopes were to be blasted by the battle of Naseby, where more than half his main army was wiped out.

The defeat there proved devastating to Charles's cause. Sir Richard Bulstrode, who had served as an officer in the Royalist army (but not at Naseby) and was reputed (inaccurately) to have lived to be a centenarian, recorded in his memoirs, published during the reign of King George I, that 'the fatal battle of Naseby ... proved the entire ruin of all the King's affairs. After the battle Charles flew from place to place, not well knowing which way to turn himself.'[7] 'After this day,' wrote Sir Philip Warwick, who had been the King's secretary, 'we may say the King's whole party fell into convulsive fits, or made strong motions, which were but indications of a dying body', while the King himself 'like a hunted partridge flitted from one garrison to another until he finally surrendered himself to the Scottish Covenanters'.[8]

In Chapters 5, 6 and 7 of this book the reasons why the battle of Naseby was fought and lost by the Royalists will be examined in detail, but first how far Charles himself was responsible for the outbreak and course of the civil war, which reached its climax at Naseby, will be considered.

1 King Charles and the Coming of the First Civil War

Several historians have stressed the need to trace the causes of the English civil war – political, social and economic – at least as far back as the Protestant Reformation in the reign of King Henry VIII, because it strengthened the position of the House of Commons (since the monarch deliberately used it as the instrument of his policy), helped to create a wider gentry class, which profited from the sale of the property of the monasteries that were then dissolved, and paved the way for the rise of a Puritan movement, destined to play a significant part in the rebellion against King Charles I.

Of course, long-term causes of historical events can always be discovered, but the idea that a formed opposition to the monarchy evolved in the House of Commons during the two reigns before that of Charles I, though at one time a popular view, has now been discounted. It is perfectly true that the monarch acting in parliament formed the supreme constitutional authority in the land, but Queen Elizabeth I and King James I held parliaments only intermittently in times of necessity, handled them flexibly, and managed on the whole to prevent the Commons from extending its authority beyond those rights that had already been attained, that is to say voting taxation during emergencies and passing legislation, usually on minor matters.

Charles's father, James I, though in many ways a comic figure because of his homosexual habits and his devotion to killing stags, was a shrewd and intelligent ruler with a sense of humour and a capacity for making up his mind quickly. He soon learned that the parliament in England exerted more influence than that in his native Scotland. He once remarked that 'he was but one king while the Commons were about 400';[1] and on another occasion after he received members of the Commons at Newmarket he called for his attendants to 'bring stools for the ambassadors'. When there was a dispute over an election return he

King James I, the first Stuart monarch in England, in a portrait by Daniel Mytens dated 1621

said he would not press his prerogatives against his subjects but 'would allow free rein to his sweet and kindly nature by confirming their privileges'.[2]

As to those who advocated the purifying of the Church of England – 'the hotter kind of Protestants' – who began to become prominent during the reign of Elizabeth I – in a conference at Hampton Court palace James granted concessions, agreed about the importance of sermons, authorized a new translation of the Bible, and fully accepted John Calvin's doctrine of pre-destination as the highway to heaven. At one stage he even consulted Parliament about his foreign policy, a subject, along with the organization of religion and the question of the succession, which were forbidden to it by Queen Elizabeth I. So, initially at any rate, King James and Parliament got along well enough together, especially when both were threatened with destruction by Roman Catholic conspirators on what came to be known as Guy Fawkes' Day.

The chief step taken by James's government which aroused parliamentary resentment was the introduction of 'impositions': these were import and export duties introduced over and above those authorized by Parliament and levied by the Customs House. In a case tried by the Court of Exchequer the judges ruled that the monarchy was entitled to levy these impositions because it had the right to regulate commerce, but of course that meant, in fact, that customs could be increased without the consent of parliament. Wisely James's government offered to freeze further impositions and also abandon certain unpopular feudal dues in return for a fixed sum to be voted to the Crown by parliament. However, this proposal, known as 'the Great Contract', was not accepted by the majority in the House of Commons, so the impositions remained a grievance. One member of parliament actually proclaimed: 'So do our impositions increase in England as it has come to be almost a tyrannical government.'[3] By the 1620s the Crown was deriving one-third of its income from impositions.

Nevertheless, such dissatisfaction was not deep enough to herald the coming of civil war when Charles's father died. But, Charles's character differed from that of his father. While James had been voluble Charles, who suffered from a slight stutter, was reticent. James was sociable, enjoyed gambling and drinking; Charles was dignified and abstemious. James was pacific, while Charles, after visiting Madrid in search of the King of Spain's sister as his bride and being thwarted and humiliated, resolved on war; he also, unlike his father, wanted to take military action to regain the German Palatinate that had been lost at the outbreak of the Thirty Years War in Europe by his sister Elizabeth's husband Frederick. Such a vast and aggressive foreign policy needed large financing and at the outset of the new reign the Treasury was virtually empty. Finally, in the hope of obtaining a French alliance against Spain Charles had concluded a marriage treaty with the young sister of the French King, Henriette Marie, and by a secret clause in the treaty committed himself to granting toleration to English Catholics who did not attend Church of England services, known as a recusants. The result of all this was that Charles's first Parliament was confused about his aims. He did not explain the size of the financial assistance which he urgently wanted nor did he disclose the name of the enemy on whom he intended to wage war, and he assured Parliament mendaciously that his marriage would bring no privileges to English Roman Catholics.

The Commons retorted by merely offering one-seventh of the help that was required from taxation and also voted only the normal customs duties, known as

Queen Henriette Marie with her eldest son, the future King Charles II, and her husband, King Charles I: a painting attributed to the Dutch artist Hendrik Pot, c. 1632

'tonnage and poundage', for one year instead of, as according to precedent, for the whole of the new reign. Charles assumed that the Commons wanted a war against Spain and protested that he had been forced on to 'new courses for the necessary defence of ourself and our people'. Somehow he managed to obtain enough money to dispatch a naval and military expedition on an undeclared assault on the Spanish fleet lying in the port of Cadiz, from which those who took part returned defeated, decimated and demoralized. Next he and his principal Minister, the 1st Duke of Buckingham, became involved in another war, this time against France, which was equally expensive and just as disastrous. The battering which the fleet underwent was dismissed as 'the youthful and unconsidered escapade of the King of England',[4] while Charles himself made no serious investigation of what went wrong and treated the consequences with the equanimity which was to become his outstanding characteristic throughout his life. He proceeded to summon a second Parliament and again asked the Commons to vote unspecified sums in taxation for unspecified purposes. Led by Sir John Eliot, a Cornish representative, the

George Villiers, 1st Duke of Buckingham, c. 1616: attributed to William Larkin

members evaded his request and, since it would then have been thought improper to blame the King himself for the catastrophes at sea, as punishment the impeachment was demanded of Buckingham, who was Lord High Admiral as well as Charles's chief adviser on foreign affairs. The King responded by ordering the arrest of Eliot and dissolved his first Parliament.

In 1627 Charles sent Buckingham in personal command of an amphibious expedition intended to attack both France and Spain, which again ended in ignominy. Next year the King summoned a third Parliament and asked for supplies. 'If they do not do their duty in this', he told members, he 'would use other means.' 'Take this not as threatening,' he concluded provocatively, 'for I scorn to threaten any but my equals.'[5] The majority in the Commons expressed indignation. They were angry that Charles had raised money by demanding forced loans from his leading subjects and had ordered the arrest of five knights who had refused to pay the loan. They claimed that the King had stretched his prerogatives beyond reason and thus attacked the institution of private property by raising money without parliamentary consent. A 'Petition of Right' was therefore drawn up and submitted to the monarch complaining that from the time of King Edward I no taxation had been levied without consent given in Parliament and that since the passage of Magna Carta in the reign of King John no subject had been imprisoned without cause shown. It also objected to the billeting of soldiers and sailors in large numbers on inhabitants of the kingdom against their wishes and to the exercise of martial law. On 2 June 1628 Charles answered that he 'willeth that right be done according to the laws and customs of the realm'. The Commons regarded the answer as meaningless and blamed Buckingham for it. Two months after Charles had given a revised and more satisfactory answer the unpopular Duke was assassinated. Thus the King lost his scapegoat.

In January 1629 Charles recalled his third Parliament. He was anxious to procure the legalization of the levying of tonnage and poundage, which he had defiantly continued to collect, although they had only been voted to him by Parliament for one year at the beginning of his reign. The Commons claimed that their collection was implicitly banned by the Petition of Right, which Charles denied, and the House was particularly incensed because the goods of one of its members, who was a merchant, had been impounded when he refused to pay the duties. However, rather than deal with this question the Speaker ruled that it was more important to discuss religion.

It was on this matter, the organization of religion, that Charles's responsibility for the coming of civil war may be deemed to have chiefly rested. Educated in Scotland, his father had been enthusiastically Calvinist, knowledgeable about theology and, although a supporter of episcopacy, had appointed an Archbishop of Canterbury who was sympathetic towards the Puritans. For his part Charles had spent all his adult life in England and took his position as Supreme Governor of the Church of England extremely seriously. The Earl of Clarendon wrote that he was 'the best Christian that the age in which he lived produced' and was 'very punctual and regular in his devotions'; Sir Richard Bulstrode put it differently: he thought that 'in matters of his religion he was always very stiff'.[6] He was not concerned over the finer points of theological doctrines, but as a cultivated aesthete he was fastidious and found the Puritans, who disapproved of paintings, images and altars, extremely distasteful. On the other hand, he would never have dreamt of accepting the supremacy or infallibility of the Pope and rejected some of the extreme doctrines of Roman Catholicism, such as the transubstantiation of the bread and wine in the communion service. Yet at the same time he declared he was a Catholic himself – that is to say an Anglo-Catholic – made use of the confessional and was not opposed to the celibacy of the clergy or the granting of indulgences. The privileges that were conferred on his Roman Catholic Queen, whose influence over him burgeoned after the death of the Duke of Buckingham, the right of Roman Catholic ambassadors in London to have their own chapels which could be attended by English Roman Catholics, and the existence among Charles's courtiers and friends of a number of Catholics or crypto-Catholics all contributed to the belief, especially among Puritans, that a 'popish plot' was being hatched at the Court of Whitehall.[7] Some of the bishops whom Charles appointed were doubtful about the doctrine of predestination as preached by John Calvin in Geneva and accepted by the majority of Anglicans, but had been questioned by a Dutch theologian named Arminius. These Arminians were claimed to be papists in disguise by those who were convinced that a popish plot was being concocted in Whitehall. Charles was not an Arminian himself, but he disapproved of theological controversies being thrashed out in the Church of England and in 1628 as Defender of the Faith and Supreme Governor of the Church he published a declaration to the effect that 'curious and unhappy differences' be laid aside as well as 'disputes over God's promises'.[8]

A sub-committee of the House of Commons at once retorted by demanding that all the laws against Roman Catholics should be put into execution, that books written by Arminian sympathizers be burnt, and that 'the authors of Popish and Arminian innovations in doctrine be condignly punished'. When on 2 March 1629 Charles, disappointed by the refusal of the Commons to legalize the levying of tonnage and poundage and their preference to devoting themselves to criticisms of his handling of Church affairs, ordered the adjournment of Parliament, the Speaker of the Commons as the King's spokesman was held down in his chair while three resolutions were passed condemning innovations in religion and the levying of tonnage and poundage without parliamentary consent and demanding the punishment of anyone who advocated the opposite as enemies of the State. The King, while insisting that he was 'not bound to give account of his actions but to God alone', published an elaborate defence of his policies, maintained that he had upheld true religion and the just liberties of his subjects against the provocations of evil men and that his aim had been to ensure 'the happiness of the nation'. As he disrobed after dissolving this Parliament, 'Charles looked pleased and declared that he would never put on those robes again.'[9] In fact he was not to summon another parliament for eleven years.

These years have been described as an eleven-year tyranny; they were not; they were years of personal rule by the King such as had been followed by his predecessors. On the whole, they were prosperous years. It is true that an economic depression occurred during 1630–1, when the King's Council did what it could to help the poor and unemployed. But after Charles had been compelled to conclude peace with Spain and France foreign trade improved, the woollen-cloth industry flourished, the price of grain fell, and therefore the real wages of labour rose, while farmers were encouraged to experiment with new methods of husbandry in order to increase their profits.

Charles's own finances were precarious since his wars had been costly and entailed heavy borrowing. To keep his head above water all sorts of expedients were adopted, some of which could be described as unconstitutional. The yields from the customs duties increased and various sources of revenue, based on obsolete feudal practices, were exploited. Some of them, for example, the draining of the fens and the sale of royal forests, injured the poor and unemployed who had extracted a kind of livelihood from them; other measures, such as fining freeholders owning land worth £40 a year because they had not taken knighthoods, the sale of patents for the manufacture of soap, and the licensing of wine sellers hit the gentry. None of these expedients produced much money. What did enhance the king's revenues was the introduction of ship money in 1635. This was a tax or rate first imposed on ports and maritime counties and afterwards extended to the entire country on the ground that everyone was responsible for the defence of the realm. It was economical to administer and was genuinely employed for the expansion of the navy. Naturally it was unpopular and was condemned as unconstitutional; but in a test case its legality was upheld by the Court of King's Bench. One of the judges cited two maxims: the first was 'that the King is a person entrusted with the state of the Commonwealth'; the second 'that the King can do no wrong'.[10] Not all the other judges agreed; and later the yield from ship money declined. Modern research has shown it not to be the case, as was once thought, that the royal autocracy was accepted with equanimity during the years after Charles dissolved Parliament in

1629. For the criticisms of his policies that had been put forward in his third Parliament were reflected in the kingdom at large.

Two points emerged during this interval between parliaments. The first is that the resentment of merchants over customs duties not authorized by the House of Commons and of landlords over the revival of obsolete feudal dues was matched by the distress felt by the poorest classes about enclosures, disafforestation and the reclamation of fenlands, which sometimes even led to rioting. Professor Underdown has recently observed: 'A general dislike of the Court and its policies from the forced loans to ship money was present in all parts of England', which culminated in 'the virtually unanimous demand for reformation of both church and state – articulated by the gentry in parliament', was 'shared by their inferiors in the provinces when Charles was obliged to recall parliament in 1640';[11] while Professor Conrad Russell has remarked that 'Charles created the union between the discontents of the parliamentary gentry and those of their social inferiors.'[12] Not everyone was happy about this temporary alliance between the rich and poor. One member of parliament, Simonds D'Ewes, was to write in May 1640: 'If the king and Parliament were not reconciled, the poorer sort will be ready to raise tumults in the kingdom and spoil the rich.'[13] The other point is that many Puritans believed that parliament was being held in abeyance and money raised by 'a party of Popish malignants around the King' in order 'to subvert true religion and the laws of England'. Robert Woodford, the town clerk of Northampton, was a typical representative of the professional class made up of clerics, schoolmasters and minor attorneys in provincial towns, who believed in the existence of such a conspiracy at Charles's Court. He associated secular affairs, like the levy of ship money and the revival of forest laws, with the cause of religion. He prayed to God 'to ease us of this great and heavy tax' – ship money – 'and grant that the kingdom would live in perfect peace and the promotion of the Gospel'. Suffering doubts about the king's godliness and trustworthiness, he feared that he was 'beset by evil men' and in 1637 expressed the hope that the Lord would move Charles to call a parliament, the only institution that would redress his subjects' grievances.[14] In fact, these two questions that emerge about the history of England in the 1630s can be linked, for the unnatural alliance between the parliamentarian gentry and their social inferiors was held together by Puritanism or at any rate the concept of a 'popish plot' on the one hand and sporadic resistance to arbitrary taxation on the other. Yet one should not exaggerate the extent of the discontent over both these matters, even though it was clearly demonstrated in Charles's third Parliament. For it did not reach its climax until 1639, when Charles resolved to make war on his Scottish subjects. Nevertheless it is perfectly clear that two conceptions about the origins of the English civil war which have been developed by modern academic historians are reasonable enough. It was a concerted movement to prevent the King from acting foolishly – or one can say unconstitutionally – and also it was a war over religion, 'the last of the wars of religion', as it has been called.

The Scottish Kirk had become Presbyterian during the reign of Charles's grandmother, Mary Queen of Scots, but his father, James I, had introduced episcopacy into Scotland, though the bishops there did not have the power or authority of those in England. Charles had a passion for uniformity, preferred sacraments to sermons, and admired ceremonious order in churches. In 1637 he ordered the introduction of a new prayer book that had been compiled by the Scottish bishops whom he instructed to 'draw up a liturgy as near that of England as might be'. Though he had taken long and careful trouble over the matter – two years were occupied in consultations between him, his Archbishop

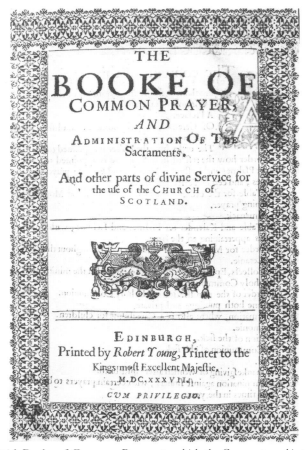

The Scottish Booke of Common Prayer, *to which the Covenanters objected in 1637*

of Canterbury and the Scottish bishops – he had not sought the advice of the Scottish Parliament nor of the General Assembly of the Scottish Kirk. They regarded his attempt to impose this new prayer book with its 'popish rites' and 'English trash' as proof that a Roman Catholic conspiracy was being contrived in London, such as many English Puritans suspected. A radical party in the Kirk planned a demonstration in Edinburgh on the day that the book was first used in St Giles's Cathedral, where women insulted the Bishop and Dean and threw stones at them. Widespread opposition to the imposition of the liturgy developed and further riots took place during the autumn. At the end of February 1638 a Scottish National Covenant was drawn up and signed by the bulk of the nation, attacking in effect the ecclesiastical policy of King Charles and pledging themselves to defend their religion, defying 'the usurped authority of the Roman Antichrist'. Naturally they repudiated 'foul aspersions of rebellion' and asserted that it was their unfeigned desire 'to maintain the majesty of our King'. Charles, however, felt no doubt whatever that the Covenanters were rebels and traitors and that their objective was to undermine the Stuart monarchy, destroy the bishops as 'the fattest deer', and rob the Church of its lands and revenues. Furthermore, he feared that if the Covenanters succeeded in disobeying him they would set a dangerous example to the Puritans in England, many of whom were Presbyterians:[15] indeed, were not all Presbyterians republicans?

Now Charles's difficulty was that he possessed no army, only a navy. He was warned that he would need 30,000 or 40,000 soldiers to suppress the disobedient Scots. So he played for time, instructing the Marquis of Hamilton, a Scottish nobleman who was one of his favourite courtiers, to persuade the leading Covenanters to return to their allegiance. Hamilton, however, warned him that if he tried to suppress the Covenanters by force he would risk provoking a rebellion in England. Nevertheless Charles set about raising an army. He called upon the service of the militia in the north of England, trusting in the hope that they would by tradition be hostile to their Scottish neighbours, and also invited his tenants-in-chief to meet him with their retainers in York. The Earl of Arundel, who, like Charles himself, was a magnificent connoisseur of painting and sculpture, was appointed Commander-in-Chief of this makeshift army. To finance the campaign the King vainly tried to borrow from the City of London. Ironically, his Queen collected small sums of money from her Roman Catholic friends, thus enlarging the dread of a popish plot.

The miliary effort, generally known as the first Bishop's War, was a farcical failure. The ill-clothed, badly armed and poorly trained men who were moved north, it has been pointed out, smashed church ornaments, the symbol of the cause of the war, on their way and helped enclosure rioters to pull down hedges. A force under the command of the Queen's favourite, the Earl of Holland, marched across the Scottish border and promptly marched back again. Though undefeated Charles felt obliged to sign a truce and on the advice of his Ministers summoned a new Parliament at Westminster in order to ask it for the supplies necessary to stage a second Bishop's War. Thus his aim to govern his subjects benevolently without calling another parliament came to a frustrating end for him. Looking back on British history it can hardly be questioned that during the years before the civil wars began Charles's conduct of social, economic and religious affairs was unwise, however admirably intentioned.

Public grievances over unparliamentary taxation, enclosures of forest, land reclamation and to a large extent religion were reflected in petitions that poured in from the counties to this short Parliament which Charles now called. Before voting him financial assistance the leading members of the Commons wanted such grievances met. Though denied the funds he wanted, Charles was unshaken in his resolve to punish the Scottish rebels and overruled his advisers who urged patience on him. So the Parliament was promptly dissolved, a new army was enlisted, and the King himself travelled to York to supervise the operations. Before he arrived the Scottish Covenanters had already crossed into England; they found their way across the river Tyne and routed the King's army. He was obliged to agree to another truce and to call another parliament at Westminster. This, known as the Long Parliament, which met in November 1640, was almost unanimous in its determination to punish the King's 'evil counsellors' for their

John Pym (1584–1643): a miniature by Samuel Cooper. Pym was the recognized leader of the House of Commons in the Long Parliament which met in November 1642

misdemeanours and ensure religious, social, economic and constitutional reforms. As the victorious Scottish army remained encamped in England Charles was compelled to assent to the demands made upon him in Parliament.

Apart from Ministers only a few avowed Royalists were to be found in the House of Commons when the Long Parliament first assembled. Men like Edward Hyde and George Digby, who were later to become leading Cavaliers, joined in the pressure for reforms. But John Pym, a sexagenarian, acknowledged to be the inspiration of the Commons, decided to concentrate attention upon the punishment of Charles's 'evil advisers'. William Laud, who had been chosen

William Laud, Archbishop of Canterbury (1633–45): after the portrait painted by Van Dyck,
c. 1636

Archbishop of Canterbury in 1633 and was the King's agent in imposing uniformity on the Church of England, was impeached for the subversion of laws and religion, as had been earlier Thomas Wentworth, a Yorkshire baronet, once a prominent member of the Commons and then appointed by the King to be President of the North and Lord Lieutenant of Ireland and finally rewarded by being created Earl of Strafford. Strafford was accused of high treason by the Commons before the House of Lords. He had, in fact, as a sick man, lacking military experience, taken command of Charles's army in the second Bishops' War and had set about organizing another army of 8,000 men, chiefly Roman Catholics, to help invade Scotland. Although he was accused of intending to use this Irish army against the Parliament in England it proved quite impossible to show that he had committed treason against his master. So a Bill of Attainder was drawn up condemning him to death and forced by a majority in the Commons upon the House of Lords and the King for signature. Charles had promised Strafford to save his life and estates. The reason why he agreed to the Act of Attainder was that huge crowds of Londoners, organized by two members of parliament for the city, demonstrated menacingly, demanding Strafford's execution. They called upon every member of the House of Lords as he went in and out 'in a loud and hideous voice' for 'justice against Strafford and all traitors'. The Commons acquiesced in these fulminations. As one member was to write: 'though Parliament do utterly dislike the rude and barbarous carriage and behaviour of the tumultuous people yet hold it fit to forebear to trouble and execute justice upon them until the kingdom is settled about again'. Frightened for himself and above all for his Queen, Charles surrendered, though he never forgave himself for doing so. On the same day that he signed Strafford's attainder he gave his consent to another Act which laid down that this Parliament could not be dissolved without its own consent.

The King's capitulation was almost complete. He agreed to all the concessions required of him, including the abolition of the prerogative courts, and admitted that the levying of ship money was illegal. By his behaviour at this stage he disclosed a fundamental weakness in his character. A strong king, like his son, the future Charles II, would have prorogued or dissolved Parliament and summoned his Lifeguard to protect himself from the menaces of riotous demonstrators.[16] Instead, all he did was to set out for Scotland in August 1641, optimistically hoping to strengthen his position there after he had made peace with the Covenanters and obtained the withdrawal of their army from England. In order to do so while he was there he involved himself in a plot – known as 'the Incident' – to put under arrest the two leading Scottish statesmen, the Earl of Argyll and the Marquis of Hamilton. This plot failed, just as did two so-called 'Army plots', which took place in England when

Thomas Wentworth, Earl of Strafford (1593–1645): a painting after Van Dyck, 1636. Charles signed the Act of Attainder which condemned the Earl to death for treason under pressure from a London mob, an action for which the King never forgave himself

partisans of the King tried to gain control of the Tower of London in the course of the year.

So Charles achieved little as the result of his journey to Scotland. Also, while he was there a rebellion broke out in Ireland, which induced John Pym and his friends to fear that if the King were empowered to raise an army to suppress this rebellion he might, in fact, use it against them. Although Charles received a mild welcome when he returned to London in November he was, therefore, presented with a Grand Remonstrance organized by Pym and carried in the House of Commons, outlining in 204 clauses 'the subversion of the fundamental laws and principles of government upon which the religion and justice of the kingdom' were established, but it was not precisely a declaration of rights. Charles promised to consider the further demands with which the Remonstrance concluded. A 'mad Christmas' followed with street battles in London. Prompted by his Queen, who thought he was pusillanimous, and encouraged by the fact that the Remonstrance had been passed by only a small majority in the House of Commons and not submitted to the House of Lords, Charles now accused five members of the Commons and one of the Lords of committing acts of treason against him and on 4 January 1642 vainly attempted to arrest them, but found that 'the birds had flown'. As usually happened throughout his life, he had acted too late. He retired to Hampton Court palace and was not to return to Westminster until he was put on trial for his life.

On 3 March Charles departed for the north of England. 'Some affirmed', he was to write later, 'that I meditated a war when I went from Whitehall only to redeem my person and my conscience from violence. God knows that I did not then think of a war.'[17] Nevertheless the Queen had earlier taken the crown jewels and sailed for Holland to buy weapons and ammunition and seek support

Charles I in armour dictating to his Secretary-at-War, Sir Edward Walker. The setting is thought to have been in the country around Nottingham, where the King raised his standard when the civil war began

for her husband there. Refusing a demand from Parliament that he should surrender to it his control over the militia, that is to say the trained bands under the control of the Lords Lieutenant in the counties, he soon began collecting soldiers and supplies for another army. In April, under pressure from the Queen, he attempted to gain control of the arsenal at Hull, but allowed himself to be defied there by a local member of parliament; in June he tried but failed to persuade the Yorkshire freeholders to promise him military support; in July he appointed the Earl of Lindsey as Commander-in-Chief of his army; finally, on 2 August he raised his standard at Nottingham, proclaiming war upon the rebels centred at Westminster. Thus it could be argued, and was argued, that it was Charles who launched war on Parliament and that it acted only in self-defence. In any case the civil war now began which culminated in the defeat of the main Royalist army at the battle of Naseby.

2 The Royalist Army

No Royalist party existed until the autumn of 1641 and no Royalist army was constituted until the autumn of 1642 when the civil war began. In peace time the only military force apart from the King's Lifeguard was the county militia or trained bands, most of which were only half-trained and not bound to serve outside their own areas. During the first six months of 1642 after Charles left London negotiations for a constitutional settlement took place between the leaders of Parliament and the King's advisers but these led nowhere. Parliament demanded that it should be given control of the militia. Charles retorted, 'By God, not for an hour,' whereupon Parliament passed an ordinance assuming its control without receiving the royal assent and appointed commissioners to take charge of the trained bands in each county instead of the Lords Lieutenant and Deputy Lords Lieutenant who normally did so. In June the King was presented with Nineteen Propositions, one of which was that he should accept the militia ordinance; other far-reaching demands included the requirement that Parliament must approve his appointments of Ministers and State officials. Charles followed advice given him by sending a moderately worded reply adumbrating the idea of a 'mixed monarchy'. Thus a kind of cold war prevailed, both sides engaging in propaganda, but at the same time preparing for real war.

Much historical investigation has been carried out recently into the questions of how the two sides began recruiting their armies, where their strengths lay, and the character of their soldiers. Charles employed a medieval practice, known as issuing commissions of array, written in Latin, the first of which was dispatched in June 1642. These enabled the King to appoint local grandees to secure the defence of their counties by summoning the local militiamen and also enlisting recruits and collecting money to pay for them. Later he found it more satisfactory to appoint colonels he trusted, regardless of their local affiliations, to raise regiments to fight for him.

A number of generalizations have been put forward about the character of the areas where the Royalists predominated at the outbreak of the first civil war. One is to the effect that neutralism – a desire to evade being involved in hostilities at all costs – handicapped Royalist recruiting; in Shropshire, for example, it is said that 'local people were unwilling to fight a war which they neither wanted nor could comprehend'.[1] One modern historian has asserted that 'the King never enjoyed much support from his ordinary subjects and even those regions usually considered most Royalist teemed with potential insurgents'.[2] Another points out, on the contrary, that Charles had no difficulty in raising seven or eight infantry regiments in 1642 not out of local militiamen.[3] A third contends that there was no popular involvement on either side because of the wide urge for neutrality.[4] At any rate, broadly speaking, Charles acquired military support in most of the West Midlands, Wales, Cheshire and Lancashire, Yorkshire, apart from the West Riding, and in large parts of Hampshire, Gloucestershire, Wiltshire and Cornwall. However, within these areas many towns, including Birmingham, Coventry, Nottingham, Manchester, Blackburn, Hull, Gloucester and later Shrewsbury, were Parliamentarian in their allegiance. It is, however, an exaggeration to say that all 600 towns in the kingdom were solidly for Parliament. Several, such as Oxford, York, Newcastle upon Tyne, Chester and Newark came under Royalist control and so did a number of market towns. It has also been plausibly argued that while nucleated villages in arable country tended to be Parliamentarian in sympathy, in pastureland, where Puritanism had only penetrated slightly, local tradition inclined people to remain loyal to the monarchy.[5]

Another popular historical generalization is to the effect that the peers and gentry supported the King while the yeomen, merchants and the poorer classes adhered to Parliament. A Venetian envoy reported in 1642: 'the King is very short of foot soldiers as the common people are enthusiastically in favour of the rebels'.[6] In fact, a number of peers, including the Parliamentarian Commander-in-Chief, the Earl of Essex, and its naval commander, the Earl of Warwick, fought against Charles, while the gentry were split down the middle, and merchants, who certainly loathed war, were equally divided. Younger sons and brothers in gentry families were, it is true, often Royalist; it has been stated that the Royalist officer corps was 'full of men who but for the civil war would have amounted to nothing very much in the world, and who suddenly had a taste of prospects open to them' and therefore 'the real muscle of the Royalist army lay with the minor gentry and their social inferiors'. It has been estimated that about one-tenth to one-fifth of the gentry families were divided in their allegiance.[7]

At first the Royalist cavalry consisted largely of volunteers. The King did not possess the resources to offer the same rates of pay to his soldiers as Parliament was able to afford. But to begin with, contributions from wealthy peers, like the Marquis of Worcester and the Earl of Newcastle, enabled the King to recruit such soldiers as did not volunteer for his service. Although when Charles raised his standard at Nottingham on 22 August 1642 he had only a few hundred men in his army, by 13 October he had 6,000 infantry, 2,000 cavalry and 1,500 dragoons (mounted infantry) at his disposal. Both sides levied taxes – assessments and excise – in the areas under their control and also sequestered estates belonging to their opponents. Certainly the Parliamentarians had access to wealthier parts of the kingdom. So in the long run the Royalists had to allow their soldiers to take 'free quarter', that is to say, pay for their food and lodging with certificates which might or might not be redeemed later. By dint of this means and other devices plus gifts and loans Charles did not have too much difficulty in sustaining and arming his men. That was essential as many of his infantry were impressed men (as they were also on the Parliamentarian side). Indeed, prisoners of war often changed sides to be sure of continuing to receive regular pay. Although when the war started foot soldiers were being given relatively high rates of pay, in some cases as much as six shillings a week, later they earned no more than ordinary agricultural labourers.

The King had little difficulty in enlisting officers, who were generally reasonably well paid, though not always punctually. Quite a number of them had experience of fighting as volunteers on the European mainland or had been soldiers of fortune. It has, in fact, been generally accepted that Charles's army contained too many officers and too few privates. Major-General Sir Arthur Aston, whose military career had extended to fighting in Poland, Russia and Germany and who served Charles throughout the civil war, complained about this in 1643, as did the members of a parliament which Charles held in Oxford in 1644. To begin with, the Royalist cavalry was superior in quality to that of the Parliamentarians. As Oliver Cromwell pointed out to his cousin, John Hampden, 'their troopers were gentlemen's sons, younger sons and persons of quality' who provided their own horses and riding clothes, supplemented by armour, and quickly adapted themselves to cavalry warfare. The Northern Horse was described as containing 'an unusually high proportion of troopers from gentry families, they and their officers being from the same region'. These troopers, who were not volunteers, were paid 2s. 6d. a day, nearly three times as much as the infantry. But as the war progressed most Royalist cavalry regiments were subject to wastage and fell greatly below establishment strength. Evidently the King had difficulty in reinforcing them.

Not a great deal is known about the training of the army. Charles was able to enlist a number of non-commissioned officers in Holland to act as muster masters, who presumably instructed infantry recruits in how to manipulate their matchlock muskets, which required several complicated movements, or handle their pikes that were simpler to use. Cavalry manoeuvres were based on Swedish practices employed in the Thirty Years War. Cavalrymen were drawn up in three ranks, advanced at a trot, and attacked with their swords, while platoons of musketeers were attached to cavalry regiments in order to meet counter-charges

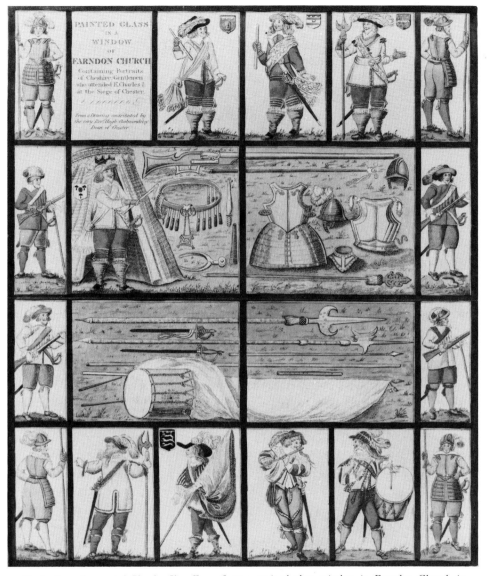

Illustration of some of Charles I's officers from a stained-glass window in Farndon Church in Cheshire

by the enemy with a salvo. Several of Charles's generals – Aston, Sir Ralph Hopton, Lord Wilmot, Prince Rupert of the Rhine and Patrick Ruthven, Earl of Forth and Brentford – had seen active service abroad, either in the Netherlands or in Germany, and had been influenced by the tactical innovations of Prince Maurice of Orange and King Gustavus Adolphus of Sweden, both of whom had contributed to a revolution in military ideas. The importance of drill and fire discipline was fully realized and many textbooks were available on the use of arms. The Royalists were rarely short of munitions and supplies. The King received imports of munitions from Holland and had small arms factories in Oxford and later in Bristol. Bullets, cannon balls, grenades and muskets were manufactured in Shropshire and Worcestershire and powder mills were established at Chester and Shrewsbury. Some weapons were obtainable from the private armouries of well-to-do gentry. A large number of tailors in and around Oxford produced uniforms, some red and some blue.

Initially the King appointed most of his leading generals for their social position and influence rather than their martial skills and gave them a fairly free hand. The only one to prove valuable was the Earl of Newcastle, who, though an aesthete like the King himself, the author of many plays and poems, wisely selected seconds-in-command who possessed a knowledge of warfare gained from service on the European mainland. The Marquis of Hertford, a bookish character, who commanded for the King in south-west England during 1643, also had the support of highly qualified subordinates. But neither the Earl of Derby in Lancashire nor Lord Herbert of Raglan in the west proved to be capable generals. In due course, however, Charles recognized the necessity of relying on experienced commanders rather than devoted noblemen. So, as has already been noted, instead of depending on leading gentry in the counties who were loyal to him, he began appointing men of proven ability without local influence to take charge of the areas where his forces were dominant. In 1644 the King appointed his promising young nephew, Prince Rupert, who had previously been in command of his cavalry, to be Lieutenant-General of the whole army and also promoted George Goring, whom Sir Richard Bulstrode described as 'without dispute as good an officer as any who served the King and the most dexterous in an emergency that I have ever seen'. About the same time Rupert's younger brother, Prince Maurice, replaced the Marquis of Hertford as Lieutenant-General in the west of England and Sir Ralph Hopton, another outstanding officer, was given a separate command in southern England. Thus, although at first Charles had favoured peers as regional commanders and nominated local grandees 'to guard the counties', his army soon ceased to be a bunch of amateurs. Indeed, by the time of the Naseby campaign the Royalist army contained many excellently officered and experienced soldiers, whereas

William Cavendish, 1st Duke of Newcastle (1592–1676), who commanded the Royalist army in the north of England, but left the kingdom after the defeat of Prince Rupert at the battle of Marston Moor: painting by Sir Anthony Van Dyck

Parliament's New Model Army which fought there included a high proportion of conscripted infantrymen.

Prince Rupert was only twenty-two when he arrived in England to fight for his uncle in the first civil war, but before that he had already been fighting as a cavalry officer in Germany on behalf of his elder brother, the heir of the deposed Elector Palatine. He had a tendency to be impatient, was often tactless and extremely sensitive to criticism, but he was conscientious and abstemious and far from reckless. However, he proved to be more successful in sieges and skirmishes than in the big battles of the war. Although the King is usually described by historians as having appointed Rupert as his 'Commander-in-Chief' after the retirement of the aged Lord Brentford in 1644, in fact, Charles himself was always the Captain-General of his own army during the first civil war and was personally responsible for all the decisions on strategy. In 1644 he gave George Goring an independent position as Lieutenant-General of Horse; and he often took the military advice of men other than Rupert, notably that of George Digby, his Secretary of State, who disliked and intrigued against the King's nephew. During the Naseby campaign, as will be seen, Charles ignored much of Rupert's counsel. In fact, he was a poor judge of character or ability and his propensity for taking the advice of the last person who spoke to him did not inspire confidence in his judgment on military matters. Men like Wilmot, Goring and Digby did not scruple to evade Rupert's orders and Charles often failed to support his nephew. Finally he was to dismiss Rupert ignominiously from his command.

The King's principal administrative body in the period before the battle of Naseby was his Council of War, which met in Christ Church College when the King was in Oxford and accompanied him on campaign. Charles was present at nearly all its meetings. Its permanent membership included his generals when they were available; otherwise the membership fluctuated, but it was also usually attended by civilians and had a civilian secretary. Its chief duties were to raise money for the army by local assessments, fix rates of pay, plan logistics, and publish proclamations. But it had limitations: firstly, its authority was confined to counties near Oxford; and secondly, although in theory it was a high-level,

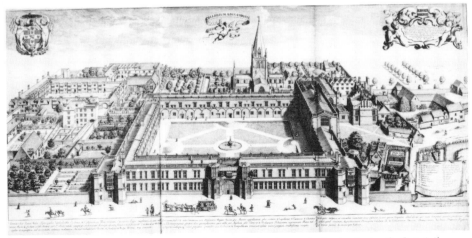

Christ Church, Oxford, where King Charles resided when he was in the city during the first civil war

strategic advisory body, often dominated by Rupert, Charles was invariably reluctant to rely on its conclusions, and in the end it became a platform for the conflict between Rupert and Digby. In the opinion of Ian Roy, the historian who investigated its work most thoroughly, 'the devious personality of Charles could not find satisfaction in a large and semi-formal council composed mainly of honest officials and straightforward soldiers. . . . The King seems to have reserved a whole area of strategy from debate.'[9]

Charles's character was, in fact, ill-suited to overall generalship, which requires toughness and decisiveness. The Earl of Clarendon, who knew him intimately, observed that the King was:

> . . . very fearless in his person, but not enterprising; and he had an excellent understanding, but was not confident enough of it which made him oftentimes change his own opinion for a worse and follow the advice of men that did not judge as well as himself. But this made him more irresolute than the junction of his affairs would admit. If he had been of a rougher and more imperious nature he would have found more respect and duty; and his not applying some severe cures to approaching evils proceeded from the lenity of his nature and the tenderness of his conscience, which in all cases of blood made him choose the softer way, and not hearken to severe counsels, how reasonably soever urged.[10]

Charles himself was to write: 'It is a hard and disputable choice for a king that loves his people and desires their love either to kill his own subjects or be killed by them.'[11] Shocked by the slaughter at Edgehill he hesitated to march on London; in 1643 he refused to storm Gloucester; and in 1644 after his victory at the battle of Lostwithiel he allowed the defeated Roundhead infantry to depart unharmed to rejoin the main army of his foes.

But the fact is, as subsequent military history has demonstrated, that wars cannot be waged in kid gloves. Oliver Cromwell was victorious, particularly in Ireland, because of his ruthlessness. Charles, conscious from the beginning of the civil war that he was fighting against his own subjects, even if they were rebels, never wanted to employ his army except to induce his enemies to surrender honourably, not to terrify them into submission. That was one of the chief reasons why the Royalist army was defeated.

3 Charles and the Civil War till 1644

When the first civil war began both sides believed that it would be decided by a single battle. Two months after he had raised his standard at Nottingham Charles as Captain-General had succeeded in raising an army of about 24,000 men, a remarkable achievement. His opposite number, the 3rd Earl of Essex, who had been appointed Commander-in-Chief of the Parliamentarian army, was a melancholy character. His father had been executed for high treason against Queen Elizabeth I and he himself had been divorced from his beautiful wife with the approval of King James I on the ground that he was impotent. The Earl had a larger army than that of the King when he left London to conduct his first campaign on 9 September 1642, but he had fewer qualified cavalrymen and dragoons than the Royalists had enlisted.

On 13 September 1642 Charles marched from Nottingham by way of Derby to Stafford; passing through Shrewsbury he arrived at Chester on 21 September, which he aimed to secure as a first priority because he hoped that reinforcements from Ireland could safely be landed there. While he was at Chester he learned that Prince Rupert, in one of the earliest skirmishes in the war, had defeated a Parliamentarian detachment of cavalry and dragoons, which formed the advance guard of the Earl of Essex's army, just outside the city of Worcester, inflicting a hundred casualties and taking over fifty prisoners. Delighted by this news, Charles returned to Shrewsbury on 12 October; he then resolved to move directly towards London, aiming to destroy the main army of his enemy, which he felt sure was bound to try to intercept him upon the way.

Meanwhile the Earl of Essex had occupied Worcester. On learning that the King was slowly marching southwards Essex planned to stop him before he neared the capital. Charles was in an optimistic frame of mind. When he arrived at Wolverhampton he sent a message to his friend, the Marquis of Hamilton, saying: 'I am expecting daily a battle; but now I think the rebels want either courage or strength to fight before they are faced.'[1]

In fact, the Earl of Essex did not lack courage, but he was delayed by the bad

Robert Devereux, 3rd Earl of Essex (1591–1646), the first Commander-in-Chief of the Parliamentarian army, who was replaced by Genereal Fairfax: a portrait attributed to Daniel Mytens

state of the roads in the autumn and the difficulties involved in carrying his heavy artillery along with him. So, although the two armies were moving more or less on parallel lines, some twenty miles or so apart, neither side knew where the other one was. Charles managed to reach the neighbourhood of Banbury, which was held by a Roundhead garrison, first. While the Royalist army was resting there Prince Rupert discovered that the army under the Earl of Essex was encamped at Kineton, a village a few miles to the north-west. Thus, by luck rather than judgment, Charles had succeeded in interposing his army between that of the Earl of Essex and his base in London. For his part the Earl had not been expecting that a battle was imminent, for he thought that the Royalists were only concerned with capturing Banbury.

It was Prince Rupert who was responsible for notifying Charles of the whereabouts of his enemy and suggested to him at about midnight on 22 October that to cut off the Roundheads from relieving Banbury he should occupy Edgehill, which sloped upwards at a gradient of one in four and lay between Kineton and Banbury. After his success at Worcester and his valuable reconnaissance of the Parliamentarian position at Kineton the King was clearly impressed by his nephew's military skill. Although he had appointed Robert Bertie, 1st Earl of Lindsey as his Lord-General (or Chief of Staff) he made it plain that Prince Rupert as his General of Horse was to be independent of him; the Prince was authorized to bypass the Council of War if he thought fit and receive his orders only from Charles himself. Lindsey had wanted the army drawn up in the relatively simple Dutch fashion (which he had learned from Prince Maurice of Orange when he served under him in the Netherlands), that is to say with the cavalry advancing in three ranks one by one. But Rupert advocated the alternative Swedish method, which meant forming up the cavalry in a diamond shape supported by musketeers. Peter Ruthven, a Scotsman who had fought with King Gustavus Adolphus in the Swedish army and had just joined Charles as a field marshal, naturally supported Rupert's view, whereupon Charles overruled Lindsey. The Earl, being short-tempered, resigned his command and said he would fight in the coming battle simply as colonel of his regiment of foot.

Thus Rupert was largely responsible for the lay-out of the army upon Edgehill. On the right he had under his own command the cavalry Lifeguard and four cavalry regiments and on the left he deployed five regiments under his second-in-command, Commissary-General Lord Wilmot. Between these two cavalry wings the Royalist infantry, amounting to more than 10,000 men, with the numbers of musketeers and pikemen about equally divided, were under the supreme charge of the veteran Sir Jacob Astley. The Royalist dragoons were put under Sir Arthur Aston. Charles was dissuaded by his generals from taking up a

The BATTLE
of
EDGE-HILL.

A stylized view of the battle of Edgehill published in the late seventeenth century

forward position with his army. Before the battle began, however, he inspected every brigade and then retired with his escort to the top of the hill: there he possessed a reserve which he could throw into the battle if it was needed.

The battle of Edgehill, which began on the afternoon of 23 October 1642, opened with a cannonade fired by the Parliamentarians and replied to by the Royalists. It was one of the few battles during the civil war in which much artillery was used, but it was ineffective. On the right wing Prince Rupert defeated the cavalry opposed to him with a furious charge, captured the enemy guns, and swept on for two miles until reaching the Parliamentarian baggage train at Kineton, which was enthusiastically plundered. On the left wing of the Royalist line Lord Wilmot met with little resistance except from infantry, and seeing Rupert's headlong advance on the right pursued a similar thrust on to Kineton.

It has been accepted that the reason for this push forward by all the Royalist cavalry beyond the battlefield was the belief that a victory had been won and that the Parliamentarian cavalry was in total retreat. But that was not the case. For the disappearance of the Cavalier horsemen from the field enabled two Parliamentarian cavalry regiments which had not been engaged in the fighting (presumably because oak trees, hedges and ditches covered the left-hand side of the ground) to counter-attack the Royalist infantry in the centre, left unprotected by any cavalry at all. On both sides the foot soldiers had already been involved in a furious struggle. Hedgehogs of pikemen supported by musketeers had fought each other hard and courageously: 'the execution', it was said, had been 'great on both sides'.[2] As the Royalist infantry lacked cavalry support the Parliamentarians had only to cope with the pikemen as the musketeers proved relatively ineffective. It was at this point that Charles intervened. His younger son, James, in an account he compiled about the battle wrote:

> All this while his Majesty was behind the foot; where perceiving the disorder they were in by the charge given them by the [enemy] horse and that at the same time the enemy's foot advanced against them, he resolved to march up to them himself to encourage by his presence and therefore prevent entire defeat . . . As he advanced, one of his footmen was shot in the face by his horse's side; after which he continued in the rear of the foot, till the battle was ended by night.[3]

Only the King's intervention and the belated return of Prince Rupert stopped the cavalry victory from being transformed into an infantry defeat.

By the time Rupert arrived back on the field with his tired and disorganized cavalrymen it was too late to renew the battle with any hope of complete success. Charles decided to stay on the hill when evening came and spent the night in a barn. His enemy also refused to renew the contest because of its heavy losses in troopers. Thus in theory Charles could claim a victory, although the casualties on each side were about equal, totalling over 1,000 killed. The King was shocked, even paralysed by the sight of so many dead. That was why he rejected the advice offered him both by Rupert and Ruthven, whom he had appointed his Chief of Staff in place of the Earl of Lindsey, killed in the battle, that he should immediately dispatch a flying column south with the purpose of capturing London before the Earl of Essex and his army could get back there. Moreover, he feared that a sudden and violent assault on the capital would alienate its citizens from him. So, instead, after Banbury had been occupied the King took up his headquarters in Oxford which remained his base and chief fortress until the first civil war ended. It was not until the beginning of November that Charles gave orders for his whole army to advance slowly towards London again.

It was not Charles's intention immediately to storm the capital he had reluctantly left in January; negotiations for peace were opened and a truce agreed upon. But the Parliamentarian forces under the Earl of Essex, having returned safely to London, together with the City's trained bands directed by Major-General Skippon, now confronted the King, who consequently took the view that the truce was no longer in force. He therefore ordered Rupert to seize Brentford, which lay on the northern side of the Thames. Here the Prince defeated two Parliamentarian regiments, but when Essex concentrated a force of over 20,000 men at Turnham Green higher up the river Charles called off his outnumbered army and led it back to Oxford by way of Reading, already in Royalist hands; here he organized the strengthening of the city's fortifications and prepared to hibernate. On 2 December he wrote to William Hamilton, the younger brother of the Marquis:

> I have set up my rest upon the justice of my case, being resolved that no extremity or misfortune shall make me yield: for I will be either a glorious king or a patient martyr, and as yet not being the first nor at this point apprehending the other, I think it now no unfit time to express my resolution to you.[4]

In this spirit he awaited an unexpectedly long war.

During 1643 the war fragmented. Neither side possessed any clear conception of strategy, being nonplussed by the fact that one battle had failed to determine the result of the conflict. Besides their main forces each side began forming other so-called armies, which were usually no more than modest contingents. Charles had such an army in Yorkshire under the Earl of Newcastle and another in Cornwall in effect led by Sir Ralph Hopton, 'a man of great honour, integrity and piety', who had previously been a professional officer on the European mainland. Another force, commanded by Prince Maurice, Rupert's younger brother, operated in western England. In addition garrisons were scattered throughout the kingdom by both sides. For example, the Royalists held Newark strongly while the Parliamentarians occupied Plymouth. Both in the north and the south-west of England the Royalists had the better of the fighting during the year.

But the principal centre of operations was in the narrow corridor curving eastwards which lay between Oxford, Charles's headquarters, and London, by way of Abingdon, Reading and Windsor. This covered a distance of some sixty miles and was then a four-day march for an army. Charles had the advantage of being able to organize raids from Oxford in a variety of directions. As early as February Rupert stormed Cirencester in Gloucestershire, thus opening up a line of communication between Oxford and the south-west, and in April he wrested Lichfield in Staffordshire from the Roundheads. The Earl of Essex moved slowly from Windsor and at the end of April succeeded in occupying Reading. Thence during June he reached Thame, thirteen miles from Oxford, and then attempted to take Islip, a village six miles north-west of Oxford. But once again Rupert dashed out and defeated a Parliamentarian detachment at Chalgrove field, lying between Thame and Abingdon. So by July the Earl of Essex was obliged to withdraw to Reading and the threat to Oxford and Charles's army was at an end.

Meanwhile Queen Henriette Marie, who had returned from her shopping expedition in Holland and landed adventurously in Yorkshire, managed in April to dispatch supplies of weapons and ammunition to Oxford; then she herself, after defying a Parliamentarian force near Newark, was met by Prince Rupert at Stratford-upon-Avon and was able to rejoin her husband in July. Immediately after this Rupert, taking advantage of the arms brought by the Queen, advanced with a poweful army upon Bristol to storm and capture the city. Delighted by this success, Charles, after consulting his Council of War, resolved to lay siege to Gloucester, thus completing his control over the west of England.

It is not entirely clear even now what Charles's exact purpose was in attempting to capture Gloucester – economic, political or strategic; each aim has been advocated by modern historians. Rupert's biographer asserted that the Prince 'would seem from the first to have had misgivings about the King's strategy'.[5] Certainly Charles was not worried about the difficulty of taking the town from the Parliamentarians; indeed he felt sure that its military governor, Colonel Edward Massey, would surrender under pressure. But he proved entirely wrong. Distressed by the heavy losses incurred by Rupert in storming Bristol, the King rejected the Prince's advice to storm Gloucester and instead sat down on 9 August patiently waiting for it to be starved into surrender. He even left the siege for a couple of days, trusting to the aged Patrick Ruthven, now entitled Lord Forth, to keep an eye on things during his absence. Moreover, he

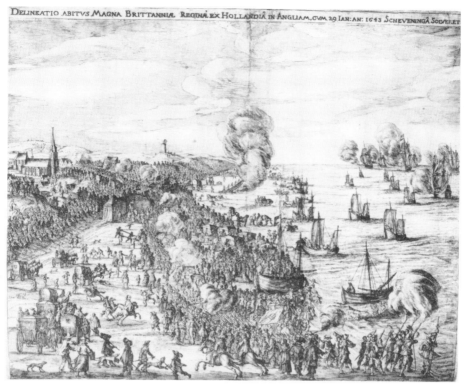

DELINEATIO ABITVS MAGNA BRITTANNIÆ REGINÆ EX HOLLANDIA IN ANGLIAM, CVM 29 IAN: AN: 1643 SCHEVENINGA SOLVERET

A contemporary illustration of Queen Henriette Marie's arrival at Bridlington in Yorkshire on 22 February 1643, bringing arms and money she had raised for her husband in the United Netherlands

neglected to build lines of circumvallation around his position which would have enabled him to hold off a relieving army. So when the Earl of Essex, pressed into urgent activity, brought his army there by forced marches, skirting round Oxford, Charles felt compelled to abandon the siege after five weeks spent in over-confidence.

As soon as he had relieved Gloucester the Earl of Essex started back for London. Charles assumed that he would follow the same route by which he came. Instead the Earl marched north to Tewkesbury but then turned south-east, crossed the Cotswolds and passed through Cirencester, where he collected valuable supplies, and then set out for Swindon, Hungerford, Newbury, Reading and London. Prince Rupert discovered what was happening and asked permission from his uncle to pursue the Earl with a force of cavalry. Charles at first refused to give him orders to do so, but at length the Prince prevailed and managed to overtake the Earl of Essex at Aldbourne Chase, five

miles north of Hungerford, finally reaching Newbury ahead of the Parliamentarian army, where he was joined by Charles's main force on 19 September.

Thus, as at Edgehill, the Royalists intercepted the Parliamentarians on the
route to their base. For that reason Rupert wanted the King to fight a defensive
battle. But Charles, presumably anxious to compensate for his repulse at
Gloucester and evidently convinced that his cavalry was superior both in
numbers and in skill to that of his enemy, again overruled his nephew. It was not,
however, terrain suited to cavalry warfare, hedges and hillocks dividing the two
lines. Although Royalist troopers attacked on both wings and were at first
victorious, the Parliamentarian infantry in the centre, consisting largely of the
well-drilled London trained bands, stood firm. The battle lasted for twelve
hours until seven o'clock in the evening. Prince Rupert and Sir John Byron, who
commanded the cavalry wings, wanted to hold on at all costs, but Charles, being
informed that his army was short of gunpowder, decided to withdraw to Oxford.
Finding the road clear, the Roundheads returned safely to London.

While the two main armies had been in contest other armies were being
formed and were manoeuvring throughout the kingdom. In Yorkshire the Earl
of Newcastle, now promoted to the rank of Marquis by his grateful master, got
the better of Lord Fairfax and his son Thomas in the West Riding, and the
Royalists had also occupied Bradford and Leeds. But the port of Hull, though
isolated, held out against all attempts to besiege it. If it is true – though this is by
no means certain – that Charles wanted the Marquis of Newcastle to lead his
victorious army towards London, it seems that the defiance of Hull and defeats
in Lincolnshire, where a new Parliamentarian army under the Earl of Manchester had been created in August, must have induced him to abandon the idea. A
second separate army, formed with the reluctant agreement of the Earl of Essex
under Sir William Waller, a skilful officer nicknamed by his friends 'William the
Conqueror', was operating in south-east England. He occupied Arundel in
Sussex before the campaigning season ended.

King Charles had attempted to raise an army to withstand Waller under Sir
Ralph Hopton, whom he ennobled as Lord Hopton of Stratton – Stratton being
the site of a notable victory which he had won over a stronger Roundhead force
earlier that spring in Devonshire. In fact, Charles had not enough soldiers to
spare for such an army and Hopton lost half his infantry to Waller, who
surprised them in their winter quarters at Alton in Hampshire during
December.

Thus, while the Royalists still dominated western and south-western England
and also most of Yorkshire, Lancashire and Cheshire during 1643, the
Roundheads controlled Lincolnshire and East Anglia as well as the home
counties and south-east England. On the other hand, in spite of their victory at

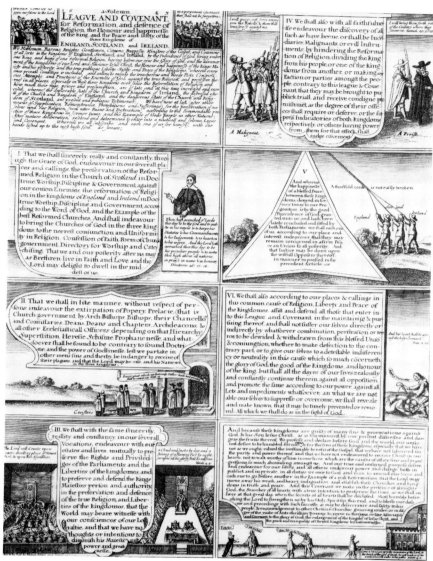

An engraving by Wenceslaus Hollar of the Solemn League and Covenant, the treaty concluded between the English and Scottish Parliaments in September 1643, whereby the Scots undertook to send an army into England to fight against the Royalists in return for an undertaking that the Scottish Church system would be adopted in England

Newbury the Parliamentarians had been obliged to evacuate Reading and therefore left the King room for manoeuvre in the Midlands. But any notion he might have contemplated of devising a converging movement on London – even if he really did so, which seems doubtful – was frustrated by his setback at Gloucester and the unwillingness of the Marquis of Newcastle to lead his army south.

In 1644 the course of the civil war changed dramatically. Concerned over the military successes of the Royalists during the previous campaigning season the Parliamentarian leaders had managed to hire a Scottish Covenanting army of 20,000 men under the command of the Earl of Leven by means of a treaty known as the Solemn League and Covenant. This committed the Parliament at Westminster to a political and religious alliance with the Scottish leaders and made the conflict a war of religion to an extent that it had not been before. Charles had been clearly warned by the Marquis of Montrose that such an alliance was in the offing, but the King had found this hard to credit after he had granted so many concessions to the Scottish Presbyterians when he had visited the country in 1641. In any case he would have discovered that it was difficult for him to do more than he actually did, which was to dispatch Prince Rupert with a sizeable army northwards to go to the assistance of the Marquis of Newcastle when he was confronted with the invasion of Yorkshire, Lord Leven having crossed the frontier into England on 19 January.

Alexander Leslie, 1st Earl of Leven (1580–1662): a painting attributed to George Jameson. Leven was Commander-in-Chief of the Scottish army which entered England in support of the Parliamentarians at the outset of 1644

Early that spring Rupert first relieved the town of Newark, which had been under siege by the Roundheads, with a scratch force he had collected. This was a quick and brilliant victory enabling the Prince to acquire a number of guns and a store of ammunition and secured this strategic town lying between Oxford and the north-east of England, which remained in Royalist hands for the rest of the first civil war. But the Royalist victory at Newark was offset by a defeat inflicted on Hopton by Waller at Cheriton, eight miles east of Winchester, a fortnight later on 29 March, and by heavy losses incurred by Prince Maurice, who had been vainly besieging Lyme Regis in Dorset. After the King had sent reinforcements to Hopton his main army in Oxford was reduced in numbers. Nevertheless a decision was taken at the Council of War held in Oxford on 25 April also to reinforce Maurice, while Rupert possessed the nucleus of an expeditionary force, consisting of 2,000 horse and 8,000 foot, which he had been recruiting, organizing and training at Shrewsbury preparatory to leading it north with a view to confronting the Scots.

The King, it was arranged, was not to act on the offensive, but to guard Oxford, Reading, Banbury, Abingdon and Wallingford with infantry while keeping a cavalry force in Oxford free to manoeuvre in support of these garrisons. It was typical of Charles's tendency to vacillate over strategic decisions that no sooner had Rupert departed for the north on 16 May than, probably on the advice of Lord Forth, he abandoned Reading, using its garrison of 2,500 men to strengthen Oxford, and a week later withdrew the garrison from Abingdon. In fact, Forth's advice was not unreasonable. Reading was of little value unless the Royalists planned to march on London, while Abingdon had no castle as a base for its defence. It was essential for Charles to concentrate his strength, since the Earl of Essex and Sir William Waller, whose combined armies outnumbered his, were now menacing Oxford. Essex was at Islip, to the east of Oxford, while Waller occupied Abingdon to the south and probed as far as the suburb of Headington. Thus Charles's headquarters was threatened on all sides. On 3 June he returned there from Woodstock and chaired another crucial meeting of his Council of War, at which the surrender of Oxford was actually contemplated. 'What!' Charles exclaimed, 'I may be found in the hands of the Earl of Essex, but I shall be dead first!'[6] Instead he resolved to ride out of the city with 5,000 horse and 2,500 musketeers, leaving only 3,500 other infantry behind. First, making a feint at Abingdon, he led his force across Port Meadow, counting on his departure to draw the Parliamentarian armies after him.

Since the King's small army was light and mobile – he had no artillery or pikemen with him – he easily outdistanced his pursuers, reaching Evesham by way of Windsor and Burford on 5 June. On 6 June Essex and Waller were at

Chipping Norton, some thirty miles from Evesham. Here they took the decision that Waller should continue to chase the King, whose strength they under-estimated, while the Earl of Essex left for Dorset to relieve Lyme Regis. This extraordinary resolution, said to have been inspired by the Earl's jealousy of Waller, was learnt of with displeasure in the House of Commons, and the Committee of Both Kingdoms, the governing body of the Anglo-Scottish military alliance, ordered Essex to return. Next day, while the Earl was still on his way to the south-west, Charles wrote to Rupert from Evesham:

> I confess the best had been to follow your advice [that is to say to have acted on the defensive in the Oxford area] . . . yet we doubt not but to defend elsewhere until you may have time to beat the Scots, but if you be too long in doing so I apprehend some inconvenience.[7]

Charles, of course, did not then know about the departure of the Earl of Essex. The King moved from Evesham to Worcester; there he stayed for a week while his tired soldiers were rested and refreshed.

Now both sides were determined on a battle. Waller thought 'the King's army

A map of the city of Worcester as it was in 1651. Charles had left Oxford for Worcester, where he was welcomed on 6 June 1644 and stayed for a week. He left Worcester again on 15 June before he defeated General Waller at the battle of Cropredy Bridge a fortnight later

was in a most discouraged broken condition' and 'if it will be well plied will be utterly broken'. 'I humbly suppose,' he wrote to the Committee of Both Kingdoms, 'if my Lord General [the Earl of Essex] would speedily advance into these parts, the work would be easy.'[8] But Essex was far away in Dorset while the King's army was in good spirits and was reinforced by pikemen and artillery from Oxford. After arriving in Buckingham and spending a few days there Charles marched towards Banbury 'to lay hold of a fit opportunity there to give the rebels battle'. On a rainy morning on 28 June an encounter battle took place between the opposing forces, the river Cherwell separating them. Waller's army advanced along a road to the west of the river while Charles's army marched east of the river, both in full sight of each other. The armies were of roughly equal size. When Waller perceived that the King's main body was a mile and a half away from his rearguard he decided to launch an attack across the river, sending two cavalry regiments supported by nine companies of foot across Cropredy Bridge and leading another thousand cavalrymen under his own command over a ford a mile and a half farther down the river, aiming to cut off the enemy rear. But the commander of the two cavalry brigades in the King's rearguard repulsed both these attacks while Charles himself, realizing what was happening, ordered his vanguard to halt and sent back his own Lifeguard to assist the rearguard. In a second charge directed by Lord Wilmot, who was Lieutenant-General of Horse in the Royalist army, Waller's forces were compelled to retreat in disorder and lost all their artillery. Altogether the battle continued for eight hours. Following his victory Charles decided against returning to Oxford, but went back to Evesham.[9]

After Charles left Worcester, before the battle of Cropredy Bridge, he had written on 14 June a famous letter to Prince Rupert giving him 'peremptory commands' to march to the relief of York, which was being besieged by three armies, that of the Scottish Covenanters, the west Yorkshire army of the Fairfaxes and the East Anglian army under the Earl of Manchester. 'If York be relieved and you beat the rebels' armies of both kingdoms,' he wrote, he himself would act on the defensive and spin out time. But if Rupert was unable to do so for any reason he had to come to the Royalist assistance at Worcester. Not unnaturally Rupert interpreted this as an order not only to relieve York but to do battle with the armies besieging it. Consequently he suffered a severe defeat by superior numbers at the battle of Marston Moor on 2 July. The letter lacked lucidity. Although some modern commentators have insisted that no staff officer today would have misunderstood these orders, it is a fact that Sir John Culpeper, who was with the King at the time he wrote the letter, told Charles: 'before God you are undone for upon this peremptory order he will fight whatever comes on't'.[10]

The battle of Marston Moor, 2 July 1644: an imaginative painting (c. 1788) by James Ward.
Prince Rupert was defeated in the battle, which took place near the city of York, by an army consisting
of English Parliamentarians and Scottish Covenanters greatly outnumbering the Royalists

Queen Henriette Marie had rejoined her husband in Oxford in mid-July 1643. There her youngest child, a daughter named after herself, was conceived. She stayed in Oxford for only nine months as she did not want her child to be born in the heart of the war zone. She therefore left for Exeter. The Earl of Essex refused to give her permission to go to Bath to recuperate after her daughter was born on 6 June 1644. So a fortnight later she left the baby in Exeter and sailed from Falmouth to her native France. She was never to see her husband again. It was concern for her safety that induced Charles after his victory over Waller to follow the Earl of Essex to south-western England because he was afraid the Earl might arrest the Queen in Exeter. His resolve to march to Devonshire was reached in the second week of July 1644. The news of Rupert's defeat at Marston Moor in any case put a stop to the obvious alternative of a move north.

The Earl of Essex had no difficulty in relieving Lyme Regis in Dorset, which had been under siege by Prince Maurice, and Plymouth, which had been besieged by Sir Richard Grenville, a soldier of fortune who had changed sides. But the size of the Parliamentarian army after providing garrisons for the towns occupied in Dorset and Devon was reduced to about 10,000 men while

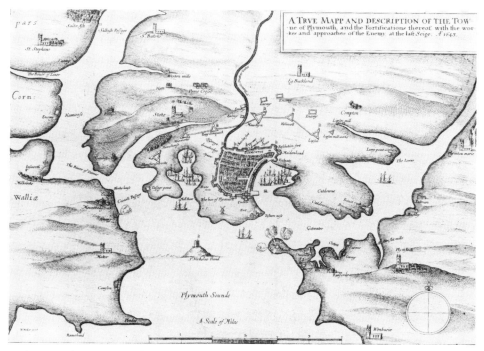

A map and description of Plymouth as it was during the civil war, when it was held by the Parliamentarians: engraving by Hollar, 1644, intended to illustrate a Parliamentarian pamphlet

Charles's army was augmented from Oxford to about 16,000. Prince Maurice had a force of some 9,000 men in Dorset while Lord Hopton and Sir Richard Grenville had smaller contingents at their disposal. These four Royalist armies were united on 11 August. Charles then vainly tried to persuade the Earl of Essex to change sides. The Earl had crossed into Cornwall, perhaps unwisely, for when he got there he reported to the Committee of Both Kingdoms that the county was 'rising universally against us with the exception of a few gentlemen'. Realizing that he was outnumbered and surrounded he promised: 'We shall sell our lives as at dear a rate as may be . . .'.[11]

During the second week of August Charles was extremely busy. He made further attempts to persuade the Earl of Essex to come over to him; he dismissed Lord Wilmot, who had served him admirably at Cropredy Bridge, and also his Master of the Ordnance, and replaced them with General Goring and General Hopton, certainly two of his most able officers. Then the King succeeded in confining the Roundhead army into the narrow valley of the river Fowey, which was commanded by hills 400 feet high on either side and stretched down from the village of Lostwithiel to the port of Fowey at the estuary of the river. The

Earl of Essex had deliberately shifted his army down towards the sea in order to establish contact with the Parliamentarian fleet under the Earl of Warwick, which he trusted was coming to his rescue. In fact, Warwick was held back by adverse winds and an army reinforcement dispatched by the Committee of Both Kingdoms was beaten on its way south-west.

The military confrontation which covered an area five miles deep and two miles wide continued for five days. The King personally reconnoitred his enemy's position and managed to conceal the deployment of his four armies

Robert Rich, 2nd Earl of Warwick (1587–1650): attributed to G.P. Harding. Rich commanded the Parliamentarian fleet which failed to relieve the Earl of Essex when he was surrounded by King Charles's forces at Lostwithiel in 1644

along a fifteen-mile front. On 30 August he learned that the bulk of the Parliamentarian army was intending to break through this long line. Though warned of the plan by deserters, he proved to be unable to prevent the cavalry, led by Sir William Balfour, who had already distinguished himself at the battle of Edgehill, from getting away in the dark on a misty night to reach the safety of Plymouth with only small losses. The Earl of Essex also managed to escape to Plymouth in a fishing boat, leaving his surrounded infantry to surrender *en masse*. Charles granted exceptionally favourable terms. No prisoners were taken. Officers above the rank of corporal were allowed to retain their arms, a Royalist escort was provided to accompany the able-bodied on their march

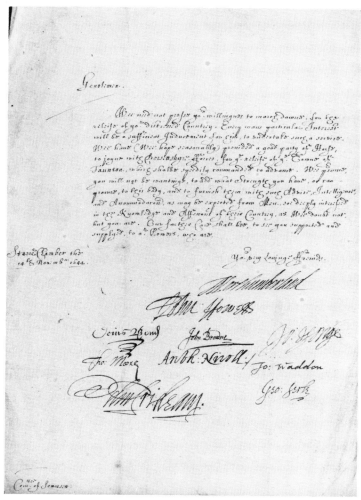

A letter from the Star Chamber relating to the relief of Taunton, 1644

through Devonshire, and the wounded were sent by sea to Plymouth. Owing to harassment by Cornish peasants and lack of sufficient food and clothing, only one-sixth of the Parliamentarian infantry survived a dreadful march away from Lostwithiel.

Thus Charles freed Cornwall from his enemy and inflicted a second defeat on a Parliamentarian army. But after his victory he failed to capture Plymouth because, as at Gloucester, he refused to storm the town. Moreover, Taunton in Somerset and Lyme in Dorset were left in the control of garrisons which enabled the Roundheads to conquer the west of England during the following year. With his superiority in men and arms Charles clearly might have accomplished more than he did. That is what Sir William Waller thought, for he warned the Committee of Both Kingdoms that 'if there be not courses taken to oppose the enemy with a strong power, I know nothing to hinder them marching to London'.

Charles had no such intention. His purposes after his victories were simply to detach forces to blockade towns garrisoned by his enemy and relieve garrisons held by his own side. In an extremely leisurely way he proceeded eastwards, enabling three Parliamentarian armies, commanded respectively by the Earl of Manchester, Sir William Waller and the Earl of Essex, with a reconstituted force

Sir William Waller (1597–1668), one of the ablest Parliamentarian generals, who was defeated by King Charles at the battle of Cropredy Bridge and defied by the King at the second battle of Newbury in 1644. Painting by Sir Peter Lely (1618–80)

of 3,000 infantry, to concentrate and impede his return to his base at Oxford. On 22 October the King arrived at Newbury, whence he detached the Earl of Northampton to relieve Banbury Castle, which was under siege. That reduced the size of his main army, exhausted after its long march back from Cornwall, to 9,000 men. The Parliamentarian armies amounted to some 19,000 men with twenty-four guns, but lacked a Commander-in-Chief, it being left to a Council of War to conduct operations. Waller was the driving force in this Council. The Earl of Manchester was far from being a brilliant general like his subordinate, Oliver Cromwell, and the Earl of Essex, who had caught a cold since his flight from Lostwithiel, did not join the Council at all.

The King's position at Newbury was founded upon a large mansion, Shaw House, converted into a fortress; his right flank was protected by the river Kennet; and to his left lay Donnington Castle, which had been occupied by the Royalists for over a year and contained valuable cannon. To the north of the King's front line stood the village of Speen, where his reserve was commanded by Prince Maurice. The Parliamentarian Council of War resolved to attack the Royalist lines both from front and rear. The bulk of its armies, including Cromwell's cavalry and a large body of infantry, therefore undertook a thirteen-mile circuitous march; at about three o'clock on the afternoon of 27 October an assault was launched on the Royalist reserve force around the village of Speen, where King Charles was with Prince Maurice. A fierce cavalry battle ensued which continued until early nightfall. The attack by the Earl of Manchester on Shaw House failed to coincide with the assault on the Royalist rear, as had been planned; in any case it was repulsed. Thus Charles conducted a successful though difficult defensive action against a much superior enemy force; and most of his own army reached Oxford safely on the following day.

Charles was now joined by Rupert, who had returned with the remnants of his army from his crushing defeat in Yorkshire. Far from blaming the Prince for his losses there Charles appointed him to replace Patrick Ruthven, whom he had created Earl of Brentford but who had been wounded at Newbury and was ageing, bibulous and gouty, as Captain-General of all his armies in England as well as retaining his post as Master of the Horse. Thus, in theory at least, Rupert was in a position to determine future strategy. But it proved too late for him to make a decisive impact on the course of events. In fact, Charles remained in supreme command of his own armies.

Three days after his appointment (on 6 November 1644) Rupert accompanied Charles back to Newbury: he then wanted the King to resume the battle against the Parliamentarians there. But Charles rejected his advice; instead he was content with retrieving the cannon and supplies from Donnington Castle, while, since the Parliamentarian higher command had disintegrated and therefore had no wish to fight a third battle at Newbury, operations came to an end.

So the campaign of 1644 finished surprisingly well for the Royalists in spite of their loss of York and much of northern England. King Charles had distinguished himself as a tactician, inflicting losses on the Roundhead armies at Cropredy Bridge, Lostwithiel and Donnington Castle. When he returned to Oxford he 'was received with the general joy and acclamation of all the people, having been absent therefrom full five months' and 'with a small force destroyed both those armies that at the beginning of the summer did so much to endanger his return'.[12] So wrote Sir Edward Walker, his Secretary at War.

Yet the King's reluctance to injure his subjects severely or endanger their property unduly was reflected in his efforts to come to terms with Sir William Waller and the Earl of Essex, who both refused to answer any of his approaches to them. Moreover, his leniency towards the infantry defeated in Cornwall, his refusal to storm Plymouth, and his unwillingness to resume the battle of Newbury were all evidence of his cautious and conciliatory attitude to warfare which contrasted with the ruthless determination of the Parliamentarian generals, headed by Oliver Cromwell, 'to prosecute the war until a full victory'. Peace terms offered to the King during the winter at Uxbridge were even harsher than those submitted to him at Oxford during the early months of the war. In particular Charles resented the demand that some of the men who had fought faithfully for him, including his nephews, Rupert and Maurice, should be excluded from a proposed Act of Oblivion. He insisted: 'there are three things I will not part with – the Church, my crown and my friends'.[13]

After his own victories in England and a remarkable campaign conducted by the Marquis of Montrose, who had been appointed by him as his Lieutenant-General in Scotland, Charles naturally rejected Parliament's terms. He looked forward to 'a merry winter'. Little did he suspect that a New Model Army, which Cromwell was persuading Parliament to create, would decimate his own army at the battle of Naseby and lose him the war.

4 The New Model Army

Although the armies fighting against King Charles had won victories in northern England during 1644, in the south Royalist progress, dissensions among Roundhead commanders, desertions and mutinies by the rank-and-file, and signs of diminishing enthusiasm for the war had depressed the militant members of the House of Commons. One orator declared: 'the Treasury is exhausted; the country is waste. A summer's victory has proved but a winter's story.' 'Our victories', wrote a Parliamentarian chronicler, 'were put into a bag with holes.'[1] The campaign of 1644 had come to an abrupt end. After the Committee of Both Kingdoms had ordered the commanding officers not to go into winter quarters during the middle of November all of them except Oliver Cromwell protested. So an air of demoralization prevailed.

When those officers who were members of parliament returned to take their places in the House of Commons Lieutenant-General Cromwell and Major-General Waller were asked by the Committee of Both Kingdoms to explain what had gone wrong during the campaign and why. They delivered a scathing criticism of the senior general at the second battle of Newbury, the Earl of Manchester. They blamed him sharply for his disinclination to continue fighting after the battle had ended to their advantage; Cromwell asserted that the Earl's backwardness:

> . . . was not merely from dullness or indisposedness to engagement, but withal from some principle of unwillingness in his Lordship to have this war prosecuted until a full victory, and a design or desire to have it ended by accommodation and that on some such terms to which it might be disadvantageous to bring the King so low.[2]

Colonel Henry Ireton, another member of parliament who fought at Newbury, testified that he had heard the Earl say that the war would never be ended by the sword but by an accommodation and that 'he would not have it ended by the sword and that if we should beat the King 99 times and he beat us once we should all be hanged'.

A contemporary portrait of Oliver Cromwell (1599–1658) by an unknown artist

The Earl of Manchester retorted by accusing Cromwell in the House of Lords of being 'inert' and 'factious' and holding radical opinions; he also condemned him for his 'animosity towards the Scottish nation'.[3] Furthermore, he insisted that all the military decisions had been taken by common consent. The Commons referred the whole question of the responsibility for the setbacks to its armies to a committee that had been appointed under the chairmanship of Zouch Tate, a member of parliament for Northampton, with the duty in the first instance of reforming the main army commanded by the Earl of Essex, which had been given an establishment of 10,000 men and promised regular pay.

A fortnight later, on 9 December, this committee reported its decisions. Tate told the Commons that the chief causes of the differences over responsiblity were 'pride and covetousness'. This broad moral condemnation aroused a general feeling in the House that mutual recriminations were leading nowhere. Tate proposed as a solution that 'during the time of this war no member of either House should have or execute any office or command, military or civil, granted or conferred by both or either Houses of Parliament'. Oliver Cromwell agreed with this proposed 'remedy', which indeed he may have originated, and came to be known as the 'Self-Denying Ordinance', on the ground that people were saying 'the members of both Houses had got great places and commands' and therefore 'will perpetually continue themselves in grandeur and not permit the war to speedily end lest their own power would determine [end] with it'. He hoped that their 'true English hearts' would inspire them 'to deny themselves and their own private interests for the common good'.[4] This splendid opportunity for self-sacrifice was eagerly and unanimously grasped by all concerned (in the Commons) ten days later. Earlier the Committee of Both Kingdoms was invited to 'consider the state and condition of all the armies' and to put forward 'a Frame or Model of a New Militia' to win the war, which it did on 6 January 1645.

Progress on these far-reaching measures was fairly leisurely and contested especially by those politicians who hoped for a negotiated peace. The Self-Denying Ordinance was rejected by the House of Lords in mid-January on the ground that it was insulting to its members, notably to the Earls of Essex and Manchester and the Earl of Warwick, the Parliamentarian Lord High Admiral. The Commons were therefore obliged to redraft it: in its final form it merely required all members of parliament to lay down their commands within forty days, but did not preclude their reappointment. It was not until 3 April that the Lords agreed unanimously to pass the revised Self-Denying Ordinance. Earlier, however, the Upper House had on 4 February accepted with certain reservations a scheme drawn up by the Committee of Both Kingdoms – on which, of course, members of the House of Lords served – for the composition of a new central army which came to be nicknamed the 'New Model'.

This army was to consist of eleven cavalry regiments, twelve infantry regiments and one regiment of dragoons, plus artillery and firelocks to defend the guns. Its total strength was to be 22,400 officers and men at an estimated cost of £50,000 a month.[5] The army was to be formed by amalgamating the remains of the three existing armies. Most of the cavalry was to come from the Earl of Manchester's army, which had been largely trained by Cromwell. Since both the officers and troopers in the cavalry regiments were relatively well paid – it was thought to be 'a good employment for a gentleman' – little difficulty was experienced in raising the cavalry. The infantry was a different matter. The three armies being drawn upon were only able to furnish fewer than half the foot soldiers needed, that is to say about 7,000 out of the 14,400 laid down by the establishment. The rest had to be impressed. That was not easy. The pay offered – eight pence a day or six shillings a week – was no more than could be earned by an agricultural labourer. Although recruits were promised regular pay, it hardly seems true, as has been suggested, that 'soldiers poured into the ranks'. When the New Model first took the field it was still under establishment strength.

On 21 January Sir Thomas Fairfax, aged thirty-three, who had won prestige in the fighting in northern England and was not a member of parliament, was appointed Commander-in-Chief of the new army by the House of Commons, although by only 101 votes to 69; on 4 February the appointment was approved by the House of Lords. General Fairfax was never a healthy man – he suffered when young from 'fits' and 'agues' – but he was always courageous and strong-minded on military matters, a strict disciplinarian who proved to be a strategist of force and quality. He was also taciturn and modest. After, on 18 February, he arrived in London he refused to be seated when addressed by the Speaker of the House of Commons, who thanked him for his past services and assured him of the confidence of Parliament during his future command.

The two Houses of Parliament agreed in mid-February that Fairfax could nominate the colonels, majors and captains who were to serve in his regiments, but insisted that they must approve his nominations, although he was empowered to select lieutenants, sergeants and gunners without any restrictions, except that preference was to be accorded to men from the disbanded armies. The Lords, reduced to a handful of peers, after considering Fairfax's list of officers for a fortnight or so, disagreed with a number on it either for political or religious reasons and demanded that the General should replace them with others. The Commons, however, firmly backed Fairfax's choices and the Lords were reluctantly obliged to give way, approving of them apparently by only a single proxy vote, and then explained defiantly on 18 March that they would 'ever be willing to concur with the Commons in what shall be fit for the saving of the kingdom'.

General Sir Thomas Fairfax (1612–71), engraved by William Faithorne after a painting by Robert Walker (1607–60). Fairfax was appointed Commander-in-Chief of the New Model Army in February 1645

General Fairfax had nearly three months in which to recruit, organize and train his New Model Army. He was supported by an older soldier, Major-General Philip Skippon, as his infantry commander, who had been in charge of the London trained bands and had learnt his trade in the Netherlands. At the beginning of April the new army was ordered to a general rendezvous at Windsor; by the end of the month it set out for the south-west of England, having received instructions from the Committee of Both Kingdoms to relieve Taunton, which was under siege by the Royalists but was being gallantly defended by Colonel Robert Blake, later to become a famous admiral. Evidently the intention was to redeem the strategic position in Devonshire and Cornwall after the humiliation suffered by the Earl of Essex during the previous year.

Besides the New Model three other armies were available to Parliament: the hired Scottish army commanded by the Earl of Leven, an English army of 10,000 men in northern England and another army of about the same size in the west. So a total of some 100,000 soldiers (including garrison troops) confronted Charles I in the spring of 1645.

Engraving of Roundhead soldiers pulling down what Puritans regarded as Popish pictures and ornaments and (below) embracing their Scottish allies

Doubt was expressed in London and elsewhere by the Parliamentarians themselves about the quality of the New Model Army they had created. It was suggested that owing to the amalgamation of the previous armies 'a multitude of good officers' had been 'put out'.[6] Joshua Sprigge, an army chaplain, who was to write an account of the coming campaign, asserted that the officers of the New Model 'were better Christians than soldiers and wiser in faith than in fighting'.[7] Sir Samuel Luke, the Roundhead military governor at Newport Pagnell, wrote: 'I think these new modellers knead all their dough with ale, for I never saw so many drinking in my life in so short a time.' He did add that the men were well armed and well paid, but also commented that the officers could hardly be distinguished from common soldiers.[8] Fairfax himself was told by a nameless 'great person' that 'he was sorry I was going with the army, for he did believe we should be beaten',[9] and naturally the Earl of Essex (who had voluntarily resigned his supreme command before the Self-Denying Ordinance took effect) and his friends had forebodings of disaster.

So it is not altogether surprising that some members of Charles's entourage disparaged the New Model Army, 'the new Noddle' as they called it, but there is no evidence that either Charles or Rupert did so. Nor is it a fact that dissensions existed in that army; its officers, it has been shown, 'covered a broad religious and political spectrum and up till the end of the first civil war refrained from political activity'.[10] Such was the character of the Parliamentarian army that fought the battle of Naseby.

5 The Road to Naseby

In March 1645 King Charles had been feeling temporarily gloomy. Peace negotiations at Uxbridge had led nowhere and, although he had offered, if both armies were disbanded, to go himself to Westminster from Oxford to continue discussions about a settlement, that did not prove to be acceptable. In the previous year he had called a Parliament consisting of his own supporters who had joined him in Oxford, numbering over forty peers and some hundred Commoners; he now told his Queen that it was 'a Mongrel Parliament' which plagued him with 'base and mutinous motions', while he had discovered that 'a great division' existed 'among his own friends upon the conditions of peace out of the universal weariness of the war'.[1]

At the end of February the town of Shrewsbury, capital of Shropshire, which was an important staging point on the routes between Oxford, Cheshire and Wales, had surrendered to a small party of Parliamentarian soldiers and thus unsettled the Royalist forces in those areas. Prince Rupert, who began operations early, wrote to his friend, William Legge, Governor of Oxford, from Shropshire:

> I fear that all Wales will be in rebellion if not speedily repressed. It will be impossible to check this business, as I am opposed by a powerful enemy, unless the King resolved to take the field.[2]

At the same time his brother, Prince Maurice, was repulsed by the Roundhead colonel, Sir William Brereton, who was besieging Chester.

However, by the end of the month the King recovered his nerve. He then told the Queen: 'the general face of my affairs . . . begins to mend . . . Montrose [in Scotland] daily prospering, my Western business mending apace, and hopeful of all the rest'.[3] In April Rupert joined Maurice in Cheshire and restored the situation there by relieving Beeston Castle, south of Chester, and later he defeated Lieutenant-Colonel Edward Massey, an outstanding Parliamentarian officer, at Ledbury, west of Hereford, a strategic town with a Royalist garrison,

Beeston Castle, south of Chester, which was relieved by Prince Rupert when on his way to Lancashire and Yorkshire in 1644. An etching by S. and N. Buck, 1727

which had called back Rupert from Cheshire to rescue it. Charles's original intention, it seems, was to meet Rupert in Hereford and march north with him to attack the depleted Scottish army now uneasily encamped in Yorkshire.

But Lieutenant-General Cromwell, who had not yet been obliged by the Self-Denying Ordinance to resign his command and had been on campaign in the west, received orders from the Committee of Both Kingdoms in the third week of April to station himself with a brigade of three cavalry regiments between Oxford and Gloucester so as to prevent a convoy of artillery being sent from Oxford to Rupert at Hereford and at the same time hem the King into his base city. First Cromwell attempted to surprise one of the King's brigades under the command of the Earl of Northampton posted at Islip, north of the city; although he failed to do so, next day (24 April) he crossed the river Cherwell and defeated the Earl, killing some twenty troopers and taking 200 prisoners. A few escaped to the nearby fortified house of Bletchingdon, but that was surrendered to him without his firing a shot. Then he harried the country round Oxford and cleared the whole area of draught horses, thus preventing Charles from leaving the city to join Rupert, as the Prince had wanted him to do, preparatory to moving north. The Parliamentarians were able to rejoice that 'Lieutenant-General Cromwell had almost frightened them out of their wits at Oxford by killing and taking multitudes.'[4] Charles, usually a merciful man, was so furious that he approved the execution of the youthful officer who had surrendered Bletchingdon to Cromwell.

Cromwell, who had 1,500 men under his command, next swept round the south-west of Oxford and tried to take Faringdon Castle on the main road to Swindon. But there he was repulsed while Lieutenant-General George Goring, an unstable character but a brilliant soldier, who had been summoned by the King from the west of England, inflicted a minor defeat on Cromwell's brigade at night. Later Cromwell was given a much larger force, with which he attempted to shadow the royal army when it moved out of Oxford towards the north-west.

On 7 May King Charles, accompanied by Prince Rupert, at last left Oxford, first for Woodstock, where they spent the night, and then to Stow-on-the-Wold, about twenty-five miles north-west of Oxford; here, joined by Goring (who had inflicted a second check on Cromwell in a skirmish at Burford), a conference was held to decide about future strategy. The King now learned somewhat belatedly that General Fairfax and his New Model Army were marching to relieve Taunton. Thus the only Parliamentarian forces that lay to the north of

Major-General Sir William Brereton (1604–61), who vainly tried to take Chester from the Royalists. The city did not surrender until 1646

him were those under Sir William Brereton, who was still besieging Chester, and the Scots, who had concentrated a depleted army against Pontefract Castle, south-west of Leeds in the West Riding of Yorkshire, which was the last outpost in northern England still occupied by a Royalist garrrison. Rupert advocated an advance northward first to relieve Chester, then to overthrow the Scots, thus avenging his own defeat at the battle of Marston Moor, and finally to open up communications with the Marquis of Montrose, who was continuing to be victorious in Scotland. Others among the Cavalier leaders, headed by Lord Digby, pressed for an immediate attack on the New Model Army. Charles now had a sizeable army at his disposal: it consisted, besides the small force with which Rupert had been fighting, of his own garrison troops from Oxford, a main body of infantry under the experienced veteran Lord Astley, a contingent of northern horse commanded by the Yorkshireman, Sir Marmaduke Langdale, and Goring's troopers. He therefore resolved upon a compromise in which, somewhat surprisingly, Rupert acquiesced: this was to order Goring, who was appointed Commander-in-Chief of all the forces in the west, to return there, tackle Fairfax and capture Taunton, while the King, accompanied by Rupert, advanced north. The Royalist army, even bereft of Goring's men, must have amounted to 9,000 or 10,000 thousand soldiers.

Meanwhile, on the same day as the conference was taking place at Stow-on-the-Wold, Fairfax, who had reached Blandford in Dorset, received orders from the Committee of Both Kingdoms (approved, as they had to be, by the two Houses of Parliament) to turn back and join Cromwell in besieging Oxford after detaching a brigade to continue westward with the duty of relieving Colonel Blake at Taunton. The exact strength of Fairfax's army at this stage is not perfectly clear. According to an officer then serving in his army, the detachment he sent to Taunton consisted of 1,400 horse and 2,000 foot;[5] but only one of the cavalry regiments and four of the infantry regiments in the New Model Army formed part of the brigade which reached Taunton, the rest belonging to garrisons or regiments already stationed in the west of England: the total must have been about 6,000. In assessing the strength of Fairfax's army at this time account has also to be taken of the fact that all the infantry regiments were under establishment size and two of his best cavalry regiments – Fairfax's own and that of Colonel Edward Whalley – had been left behind with Cromwell. Possibly, therefore, Fairfax's army, theoretically over 22,000 men strong, amounted to fewer than 15,000.

The reason why Fairfax was ordered back from Dorset was that the Committee of Both Kingdoms was deeply perturbed over the question of which way the King would decide to strike once he departed from Oxford. The Committee believed – and the majority at Westminster agreed with it – that if

Oxford were now subjected to a large-scale siege by the bulk of the New Model Army Charles would be obliged to turn back from wherever he aimed to advance in order to defend his principal military base.

As instructed, Fairfax therefore met Cromwell at Newbury and they both prepared to invest Oxford on 22 May; but by 28 May Cromwell was sent back home to Ely, merely taking four troops along with him, under orders to reinforce the defences of East Anglia in case the King's army should advance that way, while Fairfax was delayed for another ten days before he received the artillery he needed to storm Oxford which had been left behind in Reading and Windsor. In fact, the King's Council of War was not unduly disturbed by the threatened assault. 'If the Governor of Oxford assures us that he is provided for six weeks or two months,' Lord Digby wrote optimistically to Goring, 'we shall then, I make no question, relieve our northern garrisons, beat the Scots or make them retreat and march southward with a gallant army indeed. . . .'[6] Nevertheless some of the Royalist officers, particularly those who had left their wives or girl-friends behind, were agitated over the danger to the city.

Thus at this point both sides were dubious about each other's movements and intentions and were manoeuvring, as it were, in a void. Charles's decision to divide his army may, in theory at least, have been less foolish than some military historians have insisted. For early in March the King had sent his eldest son, the future Charles II, who was not yet fifteen years old, with a Council of State and an able Lieutenant-General, Lord Hopton, as his military adviser, to Bristol to take command of the royal forces in the south-west, although he was instructed 'to remain quiet till the fate of all armies could be discerned'.[7] However, Lieutenant-General Goring, who earlier had been appointed commander of the Royalist forces in the south and south-east of England and was described by Sir Edward Hyde, who accompanied Prince Charles to Bristol, as a man 'of wit, courage and understanding and ambitions uncontrolled by any fear of God or man', came to Exeter and took it upon himself to deliver orders for an attack on Taunton, although he certainly possessed no commission to do so. Nevertheless, it was clear that with the 4,500 men he had at his command, together with such soldiers as were available to Lord Hopton, Sir Richard Grenville, who had been vainly besieging Plymouth for six months, and Sir John Berkeley, the Governor of Exeter, there should have been 9,000 or 10,000 soldiers capable of fighting the brigade collected by General Fairfax and sent by him to relieve Taunton. But all these commanders quarrelled with one another. Grenville refused to cooperate with Goring; Grenville and Berkeley were at loggerheads; while Hopton took umbrage because his position was ill-defined and he would not at first consent to be involved in the siege of Taunton.

Such was the situation before Goring left Somerset to join in the conference

Charles, Prince of Wales, the future King Charles II, painted by William Dobson (1611–46). The Prince was then about fourteen. At the age of sixteen he was appointed to the nominal position of Captain-General in the south-west of England with Lord Hopton as his military adviser

at Stow-on-the-Wold. When he was ordered to return to the west by Charles on 8 May and was appointed Lieutenant-General of the whole western army, given a seat on the Prince of Wales's Council, which was told it could seek his advice but not give him orders, that did not improve matters at all. So confusing were the instructions delivered from the King to his son's Council of State at Bristol and to his generals in the west and so jealous were they of each other that

Taunton was duly relieved and remained, like Plymouth, in the secure control of the Roundheads.

Meanwhile the chief problem of the Royalist army under the King once it had left Oxford remained which way it should advance. Should it relieve Chester? Should it reopen communications between Oxford and Wales by retaking Shrewsbury? Should it enter Lancashire in the hope of gathering recruits? Should it attack the Scottish army believed to be in Yorkshire, though, in fact, the Earl of Leven was moving to Westmorland (now part of modern Cumbria), and then join the Marquis of Montrose in Scotland? Or should it turn back and confront Fairfax outside Oxford?

The Parliamentarians were equally perplexed. They did not know where the King would move next – to the north, west, east or even south. That was why Cromwell had been sent to protect East Anglia and a cavalry brigade under the command of Colonel Vermuyden had been ordered north to reinforce the Scots, who had been asked on 10 May to march speedily south. Above all, that was why General Fairfax had been instructed to return from Blandford to lay siege to Oxford, because it was hoped that this would suffice to divert the Royalists from striking anywhere at all. Indeed, ideally from the point of view of the Parliamentarians Charles's army could be crushed between the New Model Army and the Scottish army that had been summoned south.

During the last fortnight in May, therefore, the Committee of Both Kingdoms was agitated and bemused. It continued to be uncertain as to whether Charles and Rupert would move north-west through Staffordshire or north-east towards Yorkshire. The Committee took every precaution it could, dispatching a stream of orders to all its forces and garrisons. About one question it felt sure: that was since Sir William Brereton had been compelled to abandon the siege of Chester, which had been in progress for more than a year, the opportunity was open to the Royalists, if they wished, to advance into Lancashire and thence into Yorkshire whence the Scots were now known to be withdrawing.

In fact, King Charles had been following a circuitous route. The loss of Shrewsbury to the Roundheads, which was later succeeded by their capture of Evesham, had discouraged him from moving westwards. Instead, after marching through Market Drayton into Shropshire he had turned east into Stone and Uttoxeter in Staffordshire and then gone on to Burton on Trent, which he reached on Whit Sunday 25 May. Here he received two pieces of intelligence: the first was of the Parliamentarians' withdrawal from Chester and the second of Fairfax laying siege to Oxford. Charles then decided that his army might be obliged to retrace its steps to Oxford if the governor were to inform him that the city was in serious danger.

A message had already been sent to Lieutenant-General Goring instructing him to return from the west with his cavalry to rejoin the main army in Leicestershire, while later further orders were dispatched telling him to go directly to the relief of Oxford instead, in the expectation that he might be able to accomplish that without the King's help. But Rupert proposed that the surest manner of drawing Fairfax away from Oxford 'would be to fall upon some place possessed by Parliament'.[8] The Council of War approved of his advice and the King determined to besiege Leicester. Charles's army was reinforced by local garrison troops under the command of Lord Loughborough, the Military Governor of Leicestershire, and by 1,200 cavalry under the command of Sir Richard Willis, the Governor of Newark. On the morning of 30 May Prince Rupert summoned the Mayor and committee which ruled the town on behalf of Parliament to capitulate. The committee vainly tried to play for time. About three o'clock in the afternoon Rupert ordered the attack to begin. Although his main battery, which he had stationed before the most strongly fortified part of the town to the south, known as the Newark, made a breach in the walls, by six o'clock it was repaired by the garrison and a breastwork of woolsacks thrown up. The order was given at midnight to storm the Newark and fierce fighting ensued; three times the Cavaliers were repulsed, but finally they broke through and captured both of the senior Roundhead officers, who had, in fact, earlier advised the governing committee to surrender. At the same time two Royalist infantry brigades supported by horse had thrust their way into the town from the north and east where they encountered little resistance. Since the defending force in Leicester numbered only 2,070 men (of whom 900 were described simply as 'inhabitants capable of bearing arms'),[9] while the Royalist army amounted to over 10,000, the rapid fall of the town and its consequent sacking in accordance with the contemporary rules of war – although Charles did his best to restrain it – was fully understandable.

Two or three hundred Royalist soldiers were killed in the siege and others were wounded. The Parliamentarian garrison had included 440 cavalry and dragoons and 480 trained infantry; it was now replaced by 1,000 infantry not belonging to the Royalist army but raised locally from garrisons in the shire commanded by Lord Loughborough and stiffened by a few cavalry. The diminution in the size of King Charles's army as a result of the losses sustained during the short siege and the garrisoning of the town has usually been exaggerated.

Charles stayed in Leicester until Sunday 1 June. He then considered that it was his duty to return south to relieve Oxford, though that was reported to have been 'much against the will of Prince Rupert'.[10] On 5 June the King reached Market Harborough, a market town about sixteen miles south of Leicester, where he gathered up stragglers; but he now changed his mind again and determined not to continue towards Oxford unless it appeared absolutely vital for him to do so. Instead he arranged to dispatch a convoy of provisions there. One reason for this compromise was that he had been experiencing difficulties with the contingent of northern cavalrymen commanded by Sir Marmaduke Langdale, which formed a valuable part of his army; the troopers had become restless at being so far away from their homes and he was obliged to promise them that once he felt assured that Oxford was safe he would return north into Yorkshire.

On 7 June the King arrived at Daventry (twelve miles west of Northampton), where he remained for a full six days while awaiting the return of the convoy. Prince Rupert was delighted with the King's change of mind about going to Oxford – he called the idea 'a plot' that had been 'undone'.[11] In fact, before that the King had learned that General Fairfax was abandoning the siege of Oxford, but nevertheless Charles sent off the convoy of provisions, including cattle and sheep impounded in Leicestershire, accompanied by a force of 1,200 cavalrymen, because he had been notified of a scarcity of food in the city. Rupert has wrongly been blamed for this decision, though perhaps he organized it on Charles's behalf after the King had been under pressure from courtiers whose womenfolk were left in Oxford. That was the principal reason why the King remained so long in Daventry, since he needed the return of the cavalry before he could embark on his next move.

At this time Charles was certainly in an optimistic frame of mind. He passed the time by hunting and wrote to tell his Queen on 8 June: 'I may without being too much sanguine affirm that since this rebellion [began] my affairs were never in so hopeful a way.'[12] Once he was satisfied that Oxford was safe and fully stocked with provisions he meant to advance north, as Rupert had long been urging him to do. But the King also informed his Secretary of State, Sir Edward Nicholas, that the reason he remained in Daventry was not merely to await the return of the cavalry from Oxford but also 'to gather up stragglers, to learn about the movements of the New Model Army, and to prepare, if necessary, to hazard a battle'.

On the other side of the lines Thomas Fairfax had, in fact, disapproved of being ordered to lead his army to Taunton in the first place and afterwards being brought back when half-way there to besiege Oxford. On 4 June he wrote to his father, who, being a peer, had been relieved of the command he held in Yorkshire because of the Self-Denying Ordinance:

> I am very sorry we shall spend our time unprofitably before a town whilst the King hath time to strengthen himself and by terror to force obedience of all places where he comes . . . It is the earnest desire of the army to follow the King, but the endeavours of others to prevent it hath so much prevailed.[13]

However, on the very day that he wrote this letter the General received orders from Parliament giving him a free hand to march northwards by way of Berkshire and follow the King's movements as he thought fit. After three days the New Model Army arrived at Sherrington, a mile east of Newport Pagnell in Buckinghamshire, which was held for Parliament under the command of Sir Samuel Luke; there Fairfax was reinforced by the arrival of Colonel Vermuyden's brigade, which had returned from its abortive mission to join the Scots in Yorkshire. On that day Luke wrongly informed the Committee of Both Kingdoms that 'His Majesty's intentions are for Oxford and so to join with the western forces and then to march in a body on his main design' and that 'his hording [tramping] up and down since taking Leicester has been to give them room for recruiting'.[14]

Sir Samuel Luke also reported that Sir Thomas Fairfax's 'brave army' consisted of 8,000 foot and 7,000 horse and 'for number of men, horse and arms is the gallantest I have yet seen in England'.[15] Since on 10 June a trumpeter arrived in Daventry with an offer to exchange prisoners taken at Newport Pagnell for those captured at Leicester the Royalists were now absolutely confident of the proximity of their enemy. Indeed, Fairfax was marching his army through the area that lay between Daventry and Northampton anxious to come to grips with the King. By then he had secured permission from the House of Commons to recall Oliver Cromwell from East Anglia to take the vacant post of Lieutenant-General of the Cavalry in the New Model Army. On 12 June Fairfax's headquarters were situated in the village of Kislingbury, ten miles east of Daventry and five miles west of Northampton. There, at ten o'clock on the morning of 13 June, he was joined by Cromwell with 600 or 700 troopers, who were greeted with 'a mighty shout'.

Earlier that same morning (at five o'clock) Fairfax learned for certain from his Scoutmaster-General that the King's army was at last leaving Daventry; indeed, he himself spotted Royalist soldiers burning their tents on Borough Hill, just east of the town, preparatory to their departure. For Charles and Rupert were by then resolved to move away north by way of Market Harborough, where they had been earlier, in the expectation of collecting reinforcements and in the hope that Lieutenant-General Goring would rejoin them in Leicestershire. But a letter from Goring was intercepted by the Parliamentarians in which he notified Prince Rupert that he was unable to leave the west in time to help him immediately. One of the officers in the Royalist army, recording the march back to Market Harborough, noted 'its unhappy stay at Daventry so long'.[16] It lasted too long because it had enabled Fairfax to catch up with the King without difficulty and thus prevented Charles moving away quickly enough to avoid facing a battle even if he wished to do so.

In fact, when Charles left Daventry on 13 June for Market Harborough he still failed to realize how extremely close to him Fairfax was, for he wrote before his departure: 'I shall look before I leap further north.'[17] His army started off early that morning, but it is not entirely certain which route it followed. According to *A True Relation of the Victory*, a pamphlet published in London after the battle (among the Thomason tracts in the British Library), the Royalist army first turned westward to Southam, ten miles west of Daventry, then followed the road to Warwick before wheeling north-east to Market Harborough. But the pamphlet does not appear to be entirely trustworthy. The total distance would have been about forty miles. It is more reasonable to suppose that the army turned directly north-east via West Haddon, Cold Ashby, Naseby and Clipston;[18] even then the distance would have been at least twenty miles, a long march for infantry in one day. Prince Rupert spent that night in Market Harborough while Charles slept in the village of Lubenham, two miles to the west. Meanwhile Fairfax marched north from Kislingbury and advanced as far as Guilsborough, ten miles south of Market Harborough, where he spent part of the night.

Before he left Kislingbury Fairfax dispatched a strong party of horse under the command of Colonel Henry Ireton with orders to fall upon the flank of the Royalist army if the opportunity presented itself. Ireton was successful in surprising part of his enemy's rearguard in Naseby village, seven miles south of Market Harborough, while the Royalist troopers were supping and playing darts or quoits in the local inn, taking most of them prisoners. The King, who still had not realized how close on his heels the New Model Army was, learned of this alarming news at eleven o'clock on the evening of 13 June. Charles thereupon left Lubenham for Market Harborough, where he roused Prince Rupert, who was 'resting in a chair in a low room', and they called a Council of War to meet at midnight.

The alternatives discussed by the Council were whether to push on north to Leicester, where reinforcements might arrive or be collected, or to turn back and challenge the New Model Army to battle. The fear was expressed that if the first alternative was chosen the rear of the King's army, which had already been successfully attacked in Naseby village by Ireton, might be unable to escape without a severe mauling and 'if the Rear were enagaged, the whole Army might be put at Hazard; and there was no marching with the Van unless they could bring the Rear off', which, it was considered, would be 'very difficult'.[19] Sir John Ashburnham, the Army Treasurer and Paymaster, and Lord Digby, the King's Secretary of State, both extremely influential courtiers, argued vehemently that it was wiser to march back and confront the enemy rather 'than to be sought and pursued'. But, as Sir Edward Walker, the King's Secretary-at-War, noted in his

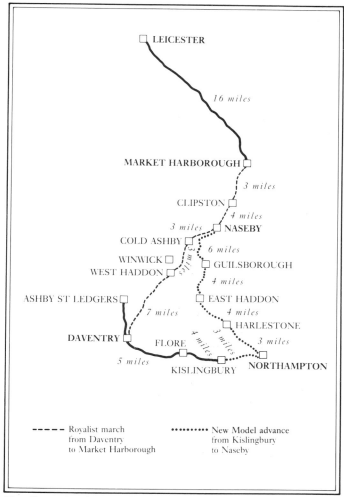

Map illustrating the routes by which the two rival armies reached Naseby

narrative of the campaign, that was said to be 'contrary to Prince Rupert's opinion',[20] although Rupert was never over-cautious or cowardly. Moreover, it appears that other officers at the meeting of the Council of War were in agreement with Rupert's view, but the courtiers won the argument. In his well-informed account of events Joshua Sprigge wrote: 'the King's counsel prevailed against the mind of his great officers, who were of the opinion that it was best to avoid fighting'.[21]

So at two o'clock on the morning of 14 June the Royalist army began mustering at Market Harborough, but it was not until after daylight at seven

Lord George Digby (1611–76), Secretary of State under Charles I. He advised the King to fight the battle of Naseby in spite of Prince Rupert's counsel not to do so

o'clock that it started to move south. Meanwhile General Fairfax had received intelligence of Colonel Ireton's victory over the Royalist rearguard and, having agreed with Lieutenant-General Cromwell and the rest of his Council of War to prepare for a battle, likewise ordered the mustering of his army. About dawn on that same morning Fairfax led his men from Guilsborough and by five o'clock they reached Naseby village. Here Fairfax obtained reliable information that the King's army was assembling in Market Harborough, but it was not yet known to him whether Charles intended to march back to the city of Leicester or to turn and face a battle. His doubts were to be quickly resolved.

'Great bodies of the enemy's horse', wrote Sprigge, 'were discovered south of Market Harborough', that is to say along a line of hills over 500 feet high which stretched for a mile from East Farndon to Great Oxendon; Walker described this as 'a rising ground of very great advantage' where 'all the army' was 'put in order and disposed to give or receive the charge'.[22] Three miles away to the south Fairfax had stationed his own men also along a row of hills, Rutnutt Hill, Fenny Hill and Mill Hill, north-west of Naseby village. In spite of the undulations that lay between the two armies, at eight o'clock they were able to glimpse each other from their respective heights. But it was not until some three hours later that the battle began.

6 The Battle of Naseby – I

What were the character and strength of the two armies which confronted each other on the battlefield of Naseby? About the regiments that took part in it there can be little dispute. Two maps – or to be more precise – sketches have survived, each illustrating the dispositions. On the Royalist side Sir Bernard de Gomme, an eminent Walloon engineer, brought over to England by Prince Rupert at the outset of the civil war and knighted by King Charles I, has left a sketch-map seemingly based on Rupert's plan of battle given to him before it took place and also embodying the New Model Army's layout. On the Parliamentarian side we possess a picture map drawn by a distinguished artist named Robert Streater (he later became sergeant painter to King Charles II and was described by Samuel Pepys as 'the famous history painter'): this was used as an illustration in Joshua Sprigge's *Anglia Rediviva*, his account of the campaigns of 1645 and 1646 dedicated to General Fairfax. Sprigge was a Parliamentary army chaplain; although it is extremely doubtful whether he was actually with the army at Naseby, his book is founded on all the pamphlets and newsletters that were available after the battle was fought. These two sketch-maps roughly confirm each other.

What they demonstrate is that the Parliamentarian army which fought in the battle consisted of twelve cavalry regiments, one dragoon regiment and eight infantry regiments. Ten of the cavalry regiments belonged to the original New Model Army establishment; in addition were a regiment commanded by Colonel John Fiennes – this may have formed part of the troopers Cromwell brought to Kislingbury – and a contingent called the Associated Horse, shown on both sketch-maps, which may also have come from East Anglia. The eight infantry regiments under the command of Major-General Philip Skippon were not brigaded: five of them fought in the front line and three in the second or rear line.

The Royalist army included as cavalry the King's, Prince Rupert's and Prince Maurice's Lifeguards, three regiments, made up of various divisions or

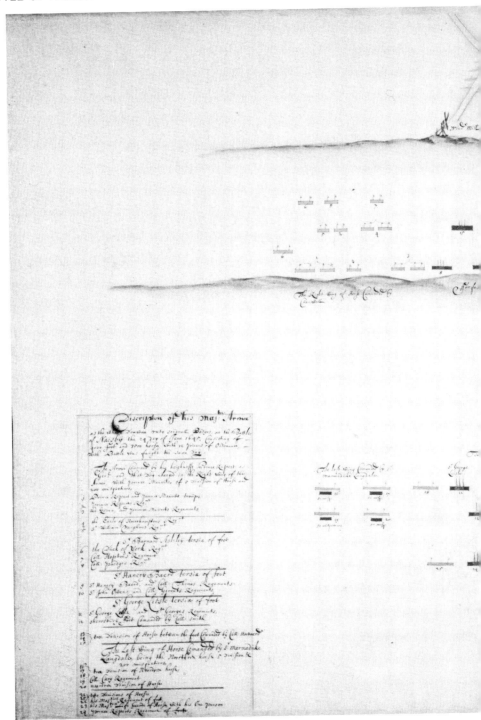

Sir Bernard de Gomme's sketch-map of the Battle of Naseby from the Royalist side

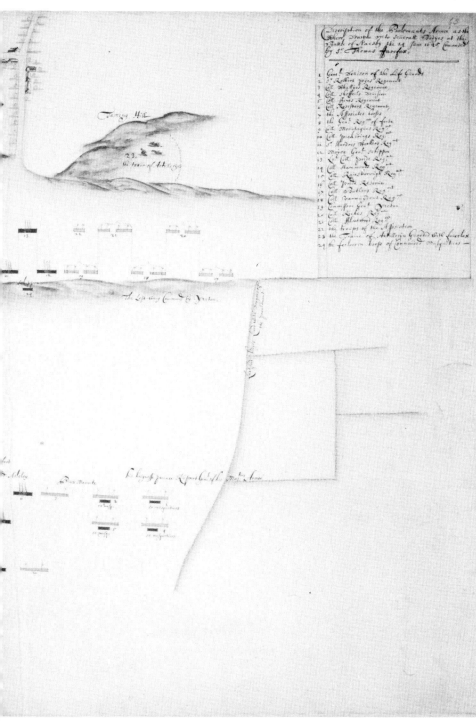

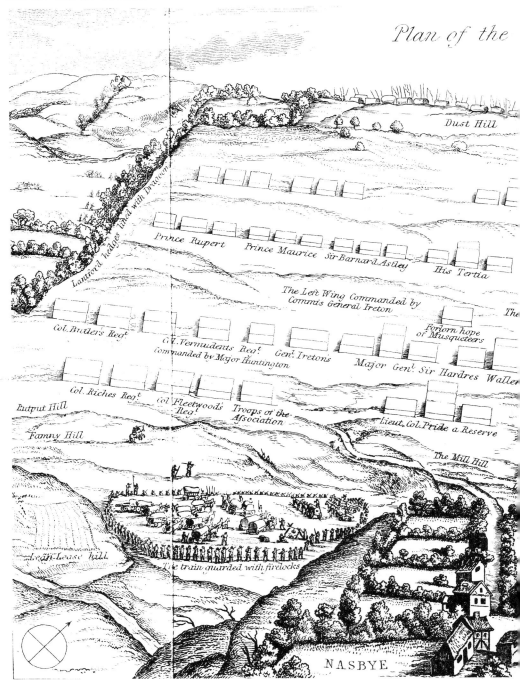

Plan of the

Dust Hill

Lanford hedges lined with Dragoon

Prince Rupert   Prince Maurice   Sir Barnard Astley   His Tertia

The Left Wing Commanded by
Comm^ds General Ireton

Col. Butler's Reg^t

Forlorn hope
of Musqueteers

G.T. Vermudens Reg^t   Genl. Iretons
commanded by Major Huntington

Major Genl. Sir Hardres Waller

Col. Riches Reg^t   Col Fleetwoods
Reg^t

Troops of the
Afsociation

Putput Hill

Lieut. Col. Pride a Reserve

Fanny Hill

The Mill Hill

Leah Lease hill   The train guarded with firelocks

NASBYE

*Robert Streater's map of the battle of Naseby as seen from the Parliamentarian side. On the left of the
village the Parliamentarian baggage train is depicted. Above, on the left wing, is shown the cavalry
commanded by Commissary-General Ireton; in the centre are the infantry lines of both sides and on
the right Lieutenant-General Cromwell's cavalry. This map was drawn to illustrate Joshua
Sprigge's* Anglia Rediviva *(1647)*

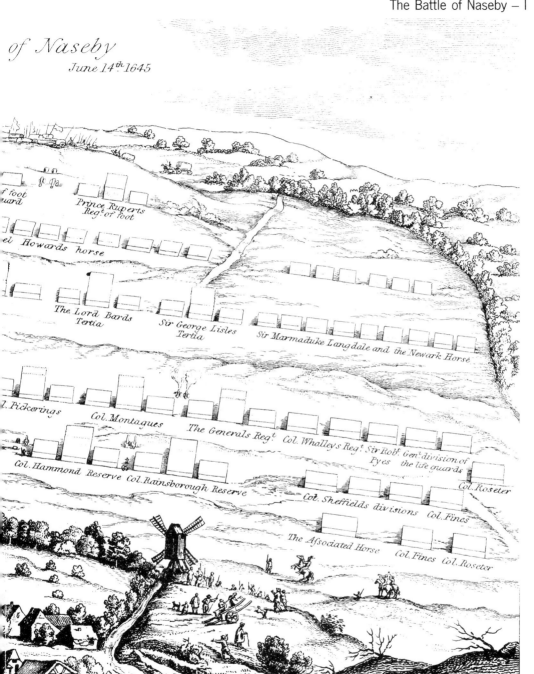

of *Naseby*
June 14th 1645

f foot
uard

Prince Ruperts
Regt of foot

el Howards horse

The Lord Bards
Tertia

Sir George Lisles
Tertia

Sir Marmaduke Langdale and the Newark Horse

l. Pickerings

Col. Montagues

The Generals Regt

Col. Whalleys Regt

Sir Robt Gent division of
Pyes the life guards

Col. Hammond Reserve Col. Rainsborough Reserve

Col. Sheffields divisions Col. Fines

Col. Roseter

The Associated Horse Col. Fines Col. Roseter

squadrons, one of which was employed in direct support of the infantry in the centre under the command of Sir Thomas Howard; the other two, which came from Yorkshire and from the garrison at Newark in Nottinghamshire, fought on the left wing; some other cavalry besides the King's Lifeguard were placed in the reserve, and a few dragoons probably also took part in the battle. No fewer than twenty-one infantry regiments or elements of such regiments can be identified on the Royalist side at Naseby and in addition groups of musketeers were employed in support of the cavalry on both wings. Another 700 foot soldiers were stationed in the reserve.

The difficulty in estimating the total size of the opposing armies lies in the fact that the number of officers and men in each formation varied so considerably. It is less of a problem to estimate in the case of the Parliamentarian army than it is in that of the Royalists; for apart from its losses at the siege of Leicester and two minor skirmishes the New Model Army had suffered few casualties between the time of its formation in the spring of 1645 and the date of the battle. Of the twelve Parliamentarian cavalry regiments only three – that of Sir Robert Pye, who himself was taken prisoner at Leicester, that of John Fiennes, which did not form part of the New Model establishment, and probably that of Sir Edward Rossiter, which was recruited in Lincolnshire – were below the prescribed strength of 600 troopers. Altogether the Parliamentarian cavalry may well have comprised over 7,000 troopers.

Of the eight Parliamentarian infantry regiments only that of Colonel Rainsborough is definitely known to have been under the establishment strength of 1,200. An estimated total of 8,000 foot soldiers is therefore reasonable. As has already been noted, Sir Samuel Luke as Governor of the garrison at Newport Pagnell was in close touch with Fairfax's army at the time it was encamped in Sherrington on 7 June (when Fairfax visited Newport Pagnell); and six days later Luke wrote his letter to the Earl of Essex in which he stated that the size of the Parliamentarian army could not be fewer than 7,000 horse and 8,000 foot, but whether the horse included Colonel Okey's regiment of dragoons is not clear.

As to the Royalist army, it is certain that all the cavalry regiments were considerably below the strength of their opposite numbers. The largest regiment was that of Prince Rupert, which contained between 400 and 500 men (some must have been killed at Leicester), and he also had his Lifeguard of about 150 men. It is true that after the siege of Leicester Charles asserted that he had only 3,500 cavalry (he had 5,600 before the siege began), but he certainly collected additional troopers from various garrisons, notably during his long stay at Daventry, and an estimate that has been made of about 5,600 at Naseby seems reasonable enough. As to the infantry, it does not appear that any Cavalier regiment numbered more than 600 men: the Duke of York's regiment, known as

Colonel Edward Montagu (later 1st Earl of Sandwich), who commanded one of the infantry regiments in the New Model Army which fought at Naseby: a portrait attributed to Mary Beale (1632–97)

the Redcoats, and Prince Rupert's regiment, known as the Bluecoats, each had about that number. There was no scarcity of officers. If one adds together the modest estimates usually assigned for the size of the twenty-one regiments which can be identified as having taken part in the battle and includes the several groups of musketeers which fought with the cavalry after the Swedish fashion, it is likely that the Royalist infantry altogether amounted to between 5,500 and 6,000 men.

We possess one estimate of the Royalists' total strength to some extent comparable with that given by Sir Samuel Luke for the Parliamentarians: this is a statement dictated by Lord Belasyse to his secretary, who wrote a brief biography of his master during the reign of King Charles II. John Belasyse, who had been elected a member of the House of Commons in 1640 and was later created a baron, was an extremely experienced officer; he had raised one of the first regiments of foot for the King, fought at Edgehill, and served the Earl of Newcastle in Yorkshire as Lieutenant-General and Governor of the city of York; he was taken prisoner after being defeated at the battle of Selby in April 1644. The King arranged for his release by an exchange of prisoners. At Naseby Belasyse fought as a volunteer in the reserve and was actually a member of the Council of War. He told his secretary that at Naseby Fairfax's army, 'as we conceived it', consisted of about 15,000 men, while the King's army was 'not exceeding 12,000 horse and foot'.[1]

Most modern military historians insist that the Royalist army did not contain in all more than 9,000 men at the outside – two of them specify 7,500 – and that it was only about half the size of the Parliamentarian army. Yet it would have been surprising if King Charles I had resolved to fight the New Model Army at such a pronounced numerical disadvantage or if, after he decided to do so, Prince Rupert had determined to take the offensive against it, even though they may have counted on achieving a surprise and have been acting partly on the belief that their infantrymen were better qualified and battle-hardened than most of the enemy's pressed foot soldiers. It is therefore not unreasonable to conclude that the Royalist army numbered something more like 11,000 men.

The battlefield of Naseby lies at the very heart of England. From the west the river Avon flows to join the Severn and Bristol Channel and from the east the river Welland runs towards the Wash and the North Sea. The land then consisted of large, open fields, partly pasture-land and partly cultivated strips, with few hedges except on the outskirts and around the village itself. The fields were ill-drained: there was much marshland and to the east the ground was dotted with furze bushes and rabbit warrens. Between the Naseby ridge and the East Farndon ridge, on which the two armies took up their initial positions, were a number of undulations and two distinctive rows of hills, those immediately north-west of the village and Dust Hill, a mile to the north, between which lay Broad Moor, where the infantry in the centre finally confronted one another. The only road across the battlefield was from Market Harborough through the village of Clipston south-west to Naseby. One of the surviving maps seems to indicate a pathway running north from Naseby to the village of Sibbertoft, five miles south-west of Market Harborough.

Of course, the landscape has now changed completely, comprising, as it does at the time of writing, small fields, trees, thick hedges and spinneys. Moreover, if and when the modern motorway is built north of Naseby village linking the M1

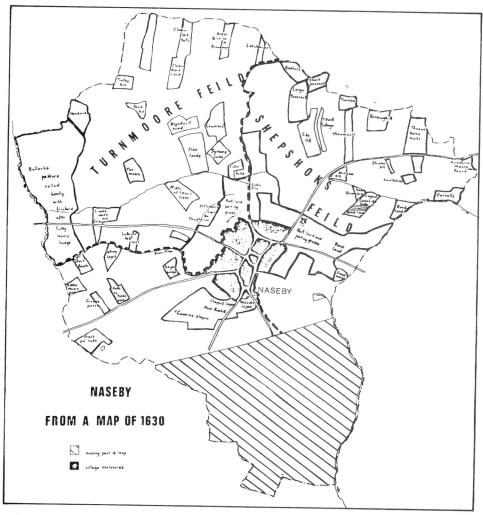

Sketch-map based on an estate plan of Naseby dated 1630 showing the roads and enclosures at that time, fifteen years before the battle took place

and A1 (to which the Ministry of Transport is committed in spite of the protests of historians) no doubt the landscape will be entirely transformed.

By eight o'clock on the morning of 14 June 1645 the Royalist army was drawn up upon the mile-long ridge which lay a mile to the south-east of Market Harborough 'and there put in order', as Sir Edward Walker wrote, 'and disposed to give or receive the charge'.[2] After prayers had been said Prince Rupert dispatched his Scoutmaster-General, Sir Francis Ruce, to seek intelligence about the exact whereabouts of the Parliamentarian forces. He returned

Photograph of part of the battleground of Naseby as it existed in 1991

to report – according to Walker, 'with a lie in his mouth' – that he had been three or four miles forward 'and could neither discover nor hear of the rebels'. Conceivably the reason he failed to do so was because after he left the East Farndon ridge the dips and other ridges hid the enemy positions from him. At any rate Rupert felt doubtful about his report and impatiently decided to take a party of cavalry and musketeers to investigate what was happening for himself. When he got as far as Broad Moor he was able to detect a movement by Fairfax's soldiers to the north of Naseby village but only indistinctly. What Rupert evidently thought he saw was a slight withdrawal south-westwards by part of the New Model Army over the brow of a hill, presumably Mill Hill (though this is by no means certain), away from the uncultivated area known as Naseby Field, where it had been previously stationed, having first moved forward from the Naseby ridge. According to one account, this backward movement from the lower ground – the so-called Naseby Field, which was boggy and therefore uninviting to a cavalry attack – had been ordered on a suggestion put forward by Oliver Cromwell to Thomas Fairfax: 'Let us, I beseech you,' he is supposed to have said, 'draw back to yonder hill which will encourage the enemy to charge us, which they cannot do in that place [Naseby Field] without absolute ruin.'[3] 'We retreated', wrote Joshua Sprigge, 'about an hundred paces from the ledge of the hill, that so the enemy might not perceive in what form our battle was drawn, nor see any confusion therein [did Rupert see confusion?], and yet we to see the form of their battle; to which we could conform ourselves for advantages, and recover the advantage of the hill when we pleased; which accordingly we did.'[4]

Whether Rupert believed that the New Model Army was actually retreating or was merely occupying a new position is uncertain, but he sent a message to King Charles 'to hasten away the foot and cannon, which were not yet come off the hill where we first made the rendezvous'.[5] The Royalist army therefore advanced from the East Farndon–Great Oxendon ridge some two miles south-west along the Clipston road to redeploy on Dust Hill, a mile and a half north of Naseby village. Both de Gomme's and Streater's maps show the whole Royalist army lined up along Dust Hill with Prince Rupert's and Prince Maurice's cavalry regiments on the right, the infantry under Major-General Astley in the centre, supported by Colonel Howard's brigade of horse, and Sir Marmaduke Langdale's Yorkshiremen with most or all of the horse from the Newark garrison on the left wing. King Charles with his reserve of 500 horse and 700 foot was stationed some distance to the rear of the infantry in the centre.

The Royalists in effect lacked a Commander-in-Chief. King Charles, it is true, had in the previous November replaced the aged and doddery Earl of Brentford with Prince Rupert as general of all his forces in England. But Brentford had really been the King's Chief of Staff and not his Captain-General; he had not been in command at the battle of Edgehill or any other battle. The King himself took all the final strategic decisions; he had, as has been noted, overruled Rupert two or three times before the battle of Naseby began, including apparently over the resolution to fight the battle at all. By giving Rupert permission, as he did, to take personal command on the right instead of leaving it to his brother Maurice, as would have been a reasonable alternative, he deprived Rupert of any opportunity to exercise supreme control. Of course, it is clear that lacking adequate maps, sufficient telescopes and watches or swift means of communication between units it was impossible for any general fully to direct the course of a large-scale battle in the civil war. But certainly at Naseby both Fairfax and Cromwell were more successful in exhibiting their tactical skills than were either Charles or Rupert.

On Dust Hill de Gomme's map shows the layout of the King's army in detail. On the right wing Prince Rupert's and Prince Maurice's cavalry regiments and Lifeguards, together with the Queen's regiment, were in the front line and the Earl of Northampton's and Sir William Vaughan's regiments in the second line; in the centre were the three 'tertias' (or brigades) of infantry under Lord Astley, commanded respectively by Sir George Lisle, Sir Henry Bard and Sir Barnard Astley; the regiments in the second line are not clearly identified, but as officers from the regiments commanded by Sir John Paulet, Sir William Murrey and Sir Matthew Appleyard were all taken prisoners in the battle these may have been the regiments involved, though Appleyard had been appointed Deputy Governor of Leicester. On the left wing only the Yorkshire horse under Langdale are shown, but four 'divisions' (squadrons) of horse, one of them under the command of Colonel Horatio Cary, appears to be indicated on de Gomme's map.[6] Sprigge's map also shows the Newark horse on that wing.

Why did Rupert select the position on Dust Hill, preferring it to the original concentration of the Royalist army on the East Farndon–Great Oxendon ridge? The latter line of deployment would have been extremely hard for Fairfax to outflank either from the east or the west. Moreover, it might have been possible for the Royalists to withdraw after a defensive battle in relative safety to Leicester. By moving his own troopers to the high ground north-west of Naseby village Fairfax tempted Rupert, as Walker observed, into 'quitting our ground of advantage' in order to advance against the enemy. Did the Prince really imagine that the New Model Army was retreating? Walker wrote that 'the Heat of Prince Rupert and his Opinion that they durst not stand him engaged us before we had turned our Cannon or chosen fit ground to fight on'.[7] Walker was an eyewitness. So too was Lord Belasyse, who considered that 'they suffered us to advance and give them the charge, which to our disadvantage we did . . .'.[8] On their evidence Cromwell was right in his contention that the Royalists would be encouraged to take the offensive.

Fairfax, who was able to see the full Royalist positions on the other side of Broad Moor, deployed his own forces in three lines so that they were tightly packed and hard to outflank. He himself, together with Major-General Skippon, drew up the infantry and 'committed the ordering of the horse' to Lieutenant-General Cromwell.[9] On his right Cromwell had so many cavalrymen – about 4,000 of them – that he had scarcely room to manoeuvre. When Colonel Rossiter's regiment joined him at the last moment he had difficulty in squeezing it in on his extreme right. Cromwell stationed his men in three lines rather more deeply than was usual because the ground was broken with rabbit holes and furze bushes. In the centre of the Parliamentarian line Skippon had eight infantry regiments under his command. Fairfax had ordered him to move his men back behind the ridge of hills south of Broad Moor so that they were hidden from the Royalists, or, as has been imaginatively suggested, to relieve them from the strain of watching the Royalists advancing across the moor upon them.[10] The result of this was that Cromwell's cavalry were slightly forward of the infantry. A 'forlorn hope' of 300 musketeers, as it was called, was posted ahead of the infantry lines, but they were, of course, ordered to withdraw if they were overrun. On the left was Colonel Ireton, who at Cromwell's request was

Major-General Philip Skippon (c. 1600–60). Skippon commanded the Parliamentarian infantry at the battle of Naseby

promoted to the rank of Commissary-General and put in charge of the six cavalry regiments. He deployed those regiments in two lines and, unlike Oliver on the right, he chose to lead the front line himself.

Cromwell, as Lieutenant-General of the Cavalry, made one additional tactical disposition. Colonel John Okey, who commanded the regiment of dragoons in the New Model Army, had been on guard every night wherever the army quartered. After he reached the battlefield of Naseby, where he began distributing ammunition to his men in a meadow, Cromwell came across the field and ordered him to mount his men and station them to line the Sulby hedges on the extreme left of Broad Moor so that they could fire upon Rupert's troops if they took the offensive on their right flank against the Parliamentarian left wing. Oliver was in a confident frame of mind; he later recalled how 'riding about my business, I could not but smile out to God in praise, in assurance of victory . . .'.[11]

Even though Prince Rupert was in an urgent hurry to assume the offensive in the hope of surprising his enemy, it must have taken the Royalist army an hour or more to advance from the East Farndon–Great Oxendon position southward to Dust Hill and redeploy in the formation pictured in de Gomme's map. The Prince drew up his cavalry on the right wing in full view of the Roundheads and, as has been noted, had to send to the King to hasten away the foot and cannon

Prince Rupert of the Rhine (1619–82): a detail from a painting attributed to Gerrit Van Honthorst

which had not yet moved from the hill where they had first amassed. Whether such guns as the Royalists possessed were fired as a signal for a general advance is uncertain, but in any case the infantry could not move at the same speed as the cavalry and indeed it has been asserted that Rupert was obliged to wait for them to catch up. The foot soldiers on both sides, it has been stated, may scarcely have been able to see each other when the contest actually began at about eleven o'clock in the morning. In his description of the battle in his famous *History of the Rebellion* the Earl of Clarendon wrote: 'the foot on either side hardly saw each other when they were within carabine shot . . .'.[12] The advance by the cavalry on the Royalist left also cannot have synchronized with Prince Rupert's advance on the right. So it was an initial charge by the troopers led by Prince Rupert that began the battle.

Charles when Prince of Wales, painted by Daniel Mytens after his return from Spain in 1623

Prince Rupert, c. 1644. Detail from a painting by William Dobson (1611–46) in Ashdown House, Oxfordshire

General Thomas Fairfax (1612–71) by an unknown artist

Prince Rupert's Charge at the Battle of Naseby, *a painting by Sir John Gilbert RA (1872)*

The execution of Charles I as depicted by an unknown contemporary artist. The medallion on the top left shows the King; that on the top right shows the executioner, who bears the features of Thomas Fairfax; at the bottom left the King is pictured being led to his execution and the bottom right shows people dipping their handkerchiefs in the blood of the martyred monarch

Oliver Cromwell. One of the many paintings by Robert Walker (1606–70). This one, painted for Cromwell's daughter, Bridget Ireton, was left by her grandson, Henry Ireton, to his nephew, David Polhill

7 The Battle of Naseby – II

The opening movement in the battle was the advance by Prince Rupert's and Prince Maurice's Lifeguards and cavalry regiments, along with the Queen's regiment between them in the front line, supported by the Earl of Northampton's and Sir William Vaughan's regiments in the second line: all these troopers moved forward on the right-hand side of the Royalist army from Dust Hill across Broad Moor to confront the left wing of General Fairfax's army commanded by Commissary-General Ireton. Ireton had Colonel Butler's cavalry regiment on his left, a regiment under the command of Major Huntingdon in the centre and his own regiment on the right, with Colonel Fleetwood's and Colonel Rich's regiments and a squadron of the Association Horse forming his second line. Ireton's men were deployed along Fenny Hill to the north-west of Naseby village; the Commissary-General had then to decide whether to draw his troopers down the hill to meet the Royalist attack or to make a stand upon the hillside.

For his part Prince Rupert first needed to overcome the musket fire from Colonel Okey's dragoons lined along the Lantford hedges (in the ancient hundred of Sulby) to the west of Broad Moor. According to Okey himself: 'My men as the enemy drew towards us . . . with shooting and rejoicing received them. . . .'[1] It is not clear whether the Royalists advanced on both sides of these hedges, nor whether the cavalrymen fired back on the dragoons, but certainly Rupert's horsemen suffered some casualties as they advanced. Sir Henry Slingsby, who fought in the battle, wrote that many of Rupert's own regiment 'were wounded from the hedge' before it encountered Ireton's extreme left wing, where Colonel Butler was in charge.[2]

Ireton now determined to lead his men 'down to the bottom of the Hill' to fight his enemies as they 'marched up in good order, a swift advance with a great deal of gallantry and resolution – coming on fast'.[3] On Ireton's left, however, neither Okey nor Butler could withstand Rupert once he gave the order to charge. Before that the Prince had halted his cavalry briefly. Why he did so is not

Commissary-General Henry Ireton (1611–1651): a painting by Robert Walker. Ireton commanded the Parliamentarian left wing at the battle of Naseby. He was married to Oliver Cromwell's eldest daughter, Bridget, a year later

certain. It may have been because the Royalist infantry was also moving forward and he wanted to give it the opportunity to catch up; but it seems more likely that he was simply dressing his lines before launching his offensive. Ireton responded by making 'a little stand also,' according to Sprigge, 'partly by reason of some disadvantage of the ground, and until the rest of the divisions [squadrons] of horse might recover their stations'.[4] At any rate the pause was not for long. On the right of his line Rupert's cavalrymen successfully overcame Butler's regiment, wounding both the colonel and the major, and 'bore down all before them' (as Walker wrote), though having to advance uphill, and captured half a dozen of the Roundheads' guns, even while Okey's dragoons were still in position firing away; Okey recorded: 'had not we by God's providence been there, there had been but few of Colonel Butler's regiment left'.[5]

On Rupert's left Ireton's and Huntingdon's regiments held up the advance of the Queen's regiment and Prince Maurice's regiment, so that the odds were about even. At this point however Ireton made a mistake. Thinking that he had managed to stem the Royalist offensive all along his front, he turned his attention to the infantry battle that had developed on his right. He therefore led his own cavalry regiment to the assistance of Skippon's infantry. But his horse was shot under him, a pike ran him through the thigh, a halberd slashed his face, and for a time he was taken prisoner. He was able to escape, but meanwhile Rupert and Maurice had penetrated his second line. Part of the Parliamentarian left wing started to retreat from the battlefield, so that Rupert and his brother were able to push on for a mile or two until they reached their enemy's baggage train, stationed to the west of Naseby village.

At the same time in the centre Major-General Lord Astley had launched his three infantry brigades across Broad Moor to confront the eight infantry regiments under Major-General Skippon, which, as has been noted, had been deployed by General Fairfax himself along the ridge of a hill to the front of Naseby village. Since the Roundheads outnumbered the Cavaliers, the Royalist infantry line was shorter than that of their opponents, which stretched along a frontage of about 1,500 yards, overlapping the Royalists on the right, where Fairfax's own regiment was in position: this overlap is clearly depicted on both the sketch-maps of the battle. After Skippon's men came over the brow of Mill Hill to meet Astley's advance the two sides exchanged only a single volley of musket fire before falling on each other at push of pike and butt-ends of their muskets.

In this contest between the infantrymen in the centre of the field the Cavaliers in spite of their numerical inferiority were at first victorious. There are three explanations for this. In the first place Skippon was wounded in the ribs by a musket shot; he had neither a second-in-command nor any brigadiers so that

The infantry who fought on both sides at the battle of Naseby consisted of musketeers and pikemen.
This illustration shows models of a pikeman (left) and a musketeer (right)

the command structure was virtually non-existent. A rumour spread that the Major-General had been killed, thus undermining the morale of his men. Secondly, the Parliamentarian foot soldiers had been surprised not only by the swiftness of the Royalists' advance but also by their tactics of merely firing their muskets once and then charging forward headed by their pikemen. Lastly, the Parliamentarian left-hand infantry regiments had been formed out of weak units from the beaten armies of Essex and Manchester while other infantrymen were pressed men who had been inadequately trained. Still, as Sprigge recorded:

. . . the colonels and officers, doing the duty of very gallant men, in endeavouring to keep their men from disorder and finding their attempts fruitless then fell into their reserves with their colours, choosing rather to fight and die than to quit the ground they stood on.[5]

General Fairfax now came to the rescue of his infantry and threw in three regiments from his reserve which, according to Sprigge, 'repelled the enemy, forcing them into a disorderly retreat'.[6] Surely this was an exaggeration. What really happened was that the Parliamentarian second infantry line advanced on to Broad Moor away from the hilly ground where the fighting had started and regrouped. Together with Fairfax's own infantry regiment, which was still intact, they mustered some 4,000 men along their new line. It was here that Fairfax took over the command. Moreover, Skippon, in spite of his severe wounds, refused to leave the field, though Fairfax urged him to do so, declaring 'he would not stir so long as a man should stand'. Thus, after a temporary period of setback and confusion, the Parliamentarian infantry redeployed on open ground and was able to extract full advantage from its numerical superiority. For their part the Royalist infantry fought 'most manfully' for two hours or more, but quite a few were killed by musket fire from the second Roundhead line.

What part, one wonders, was played by Colonel Howard's cavalry brigade, which is stated in secondary accounts of the battle to have been employed in support of Major-General Lord Astley's foot? They are described as being 'a mixed bag', for three at least of the divisions or squadrons in the brigade having spent their time on garrison duties can have been little accustomed to manoeuvres in a large formation.[7] Another account avers that two of the squadrons supported the first infantry line and one squadron supported the second. A third account simply states that Howard's brigade was interspersed with the Royalist infantry. That surely was most unusual. But really nothing positive is known. It is true that de Gomme's sketch-map shows the interspersion, but Streater's merely places 'Colonel Howard's horse' immediately to the front of the King's reserve. The most likely explanation is that the brigade was intended to assist the Royalist infantry if it was driven back, but no evidence can be found to prove that it did so. In fact, the complaint was to be made that the Royalist infantry line was left 'naked'.

While the Royalist foot soldiers fought heroically but vainly, Prince Rupert, having defeated Colonel Butler's regiment, and accompanied by his brother, reached the Parliamentarian baggage train with their cavalry. The train occupied a large area and may have contained a thousand waggons; it was stationed just north of Carvell's Lane, the only road of any consequence south of Naseby village. It was protected by firelocks and was only open to attack from the west. Rupert summoned the guard in charge of the train to surrender, but, according to Joshua Sprigge, 'it fired with admirable courage on the Prince's horse' and refused to yield.[8] It has been hazarded that Sprigge was actually with the train himself. It that was so, his is a first-class report on the episode.

When Sprigge studied the contemporary accounts of the battle he wrote: 'it is hard to say whether [which] wing of our horse charged first'.[9] But it seems reasonably certain that the action on the Parliamentarian left wing, where Ireton defended himself against Rupert's offensive, and the infantry battle in the centre both began before Cromwell on the right-hand side of the Parliamentarian line made his first move. For Cromwell's troopers were stretched across the Naseby–Clipston road, where the ground was uneven, covered with furze bushes and rabbit warrens; the exact position of his front line must have been just north-west of this road on the hills called Thornehill and Scrawhill marked on the 1630 estate map. When Sir Marmaduke Langdale with his own Yorkshire cavalry, supported by the horse from Newark, obeyed the general order to take the offensive and therefore advanced on the Royalist left, he was obliged to ride uphill. Cromwell did not think 'it fit to stand and receive the enemies' charge' and in spite of the difficulty of the terrain ordered his front line forward.[10] His battle cry was 'God our strength' while that of the Cavaliers was 'Queen Mary'. On the left of Cromwell's front line Colonel Whalley's squadrons riding downhill drove back Langdale's troopers, who after making 'a very gallant resistance' (again according to Sprigge) 'and firing at very close range, they came to the sword'.[11] They were soon compelled to retire and seek the shelter and help of Prince Rupert's foot regiment – the Bluecoats – in the King's reserve.

Cromwell now threw in Colonel Sheffield's regiment from his second line on the left and Colonel Rossiter's regiment on the extreme right. Thus the Royalist left wing was outflanked on both sides and though Cromwell himself reported how severe the struggle was and Walker wrote that the Cavaliers 'did as well as the Place and their Number would admit' the Earl of Clarendon was to observe nastily that they 'fled further and faster than became them'.[12] Possibly the cavalry advanced too wide of their front, but they had been compelled to attack superior numbers uphill and it is scarcely surprising that in the end they retreated in disorder.

By now the infantry battle had been resumed on Broad Moor. Astley's second infantry line had regrouped on open ground to engage in a last stand against the New Model foot, which, after its destruction of the Royalist front line, was also regrouping. But Cromwell then decided to intervene in the infantry battle just as he had done on Marston Moor; he was also anxious to prevent the Royalist cavalry (as Sprigge noted) from coming to the rescue of their infantry. So, leaving it to Whalley's and Sheffield's regiments to thrust back Langdale's beaten troopers, Cromwell ordered the bulk of his cavalry to attack the Royalist

Sir Marmaduke Langdale (1598–1662), who commanded the Royalist cavalry on the left wing at the battle of Naseby, where he was defeated by Oliver Cromwell

foot soldiers who were fighting back again at push of pike. On the left-hand side of the battlefield Colonel Okey perceived what was happening (according to his own account the battle had then lasted for one hour) so he resolved to mount his dragoons and charge the Royalist foot on their right. Furthermore Commissary-General Ireton summoned the remains of his cavalry wing also to join the assault on the surviving Cavalier infantry by crossing the Moor to occupy Cromwell's original position where he began his offensive. Thus (to quote Colonel Rogers), 'attacked in the flank and rear by the horse, the valiant regiments of infantry which had served the King so well in so many campaigns were now giving way'. One of the three brigades under Astley's command – probably that led by Colonel Lisle – continued to fight on, again in the words of Sprigge 'with incredible courage and resolution', but was finally defeated by Fairfax's own regiment of foot and Lifeguard of horse, which charged it both from front and rear. By then the rest of the Royalist infantry had laid down their arms in return for the promise of mercy. Okey's dragoons alone took 500 prisoners.

The two questions that stand out in the last confusing stage of the battle are: what part was played by King Charles with his reserve and why was Prince Rupert, when he returned to the field after his humiliation at the Parliament-arian baggage train, unable to rally the forces that survived? So far as the King is concerned the problem is what the exact strength of the reserve was that he had at his disposal. It has been suggested that he had as many as 1,500 horse and 800 foot, which was certainly as large a reserve as Cromwell was to have at the battles of Dunbar and Worcester. According to de Gomme's sketch-map it included the King's Lifeguard of horse, which at Leicester numbered only 130 men, though it has been said to have amounted on that day to 500 guardsmen, a remarkably high figure; the Lifeguard of foot, which contained 200 or 300 men; Prince Rupert's regiment of foot, which had numbered 400 at Leicester, but suffered losses there; and possibly the Newark horse plus some musketeers. However, it is extremely doubtful if any of the Newark horse were in the reserve: these cavalrymen appear mainly to have fought with Langdale's men on the Royalist left wing, while the Bluecoats were already heavily engaged by Cromwell's troopers when Langdale's men withdrew to shelter behind them. So, in fact, the reserve that King Charles had at his command is not likely to have consisted of more than 1,000 men, unless part of Colonel Howard's brigade was still intact. In any case, in the words of the Earl of Clarendon, who based his account on Walker's *Brief Memorials*:

The King's reserve of horse – which was his own guards with himself at the head of them – was even ready to charge the enemy horse who followed those of the left wing when, on a sudden, such a panic seized upon them that they all ran near a quarter of a mile without stopping . . . However, the Earl of Carnwath, who rode next to him (a man never suspected of infidelity, nor one from whom the King would have received counsel in such a case) on a sudden laid his hand on the bridle of the King's horse, and swearing two or three full-mouthed Scot's oaths . . . said 'Will you ride upon your death in an instant?'[12]

This created utter confusion. The Earl turned the King's horse round, which made the troopers believe they had been ordered to march to the right, away from the enemy. 'So,' wrote Clarendon, 'they all turned their horses and rode upon the spur, as if they were every man to shift for himself,' though some of them stood firm.[13] Still it is likely that Carnwath's action saved the King's life. Romantic biographers have argued, however, that it would have been nobler and more heroic if Charles had fought and died on the battlefield rather than suffer the indignity of being executed on the scaffold three and a half years later.

It was at this stage, after the battle had been in progress for nearly three hours, that Prince Rupert and his cavalrymen came back to the battlefield and joined the King at the top of Broad Moor. Neither of them was able to arouse any

A contemporary engraving of the battle of Naseby depicting the occasion when the Earl of Carnwath turned away the King's horse when Charles was about to throw in his reserve, saying, 'Will you go upon your death this instant?' and thus impeded the counter-charge against the victorious Roundheads

inspiration in the broken troops, consisting of the King's Lifeguard, the beaten Yorkshire horsemen under Langdale, and Rupert's own men, exhausted by their exertions. None could prevail 'with those scattered or frightened troops either to give or stand one charge more'.[14] So related Lord Belasyse, one of the courtiers who was on the spot with King Charles. Walker adds: 'After all the endeavours of the King and Prince Rupert to the hazard of their persons they were fain to quit the field and leave Fairfax Master of all our Foot, Cannon, Baggage and Plunder taken at Leicester.' Cromwell's troopers chased after the retreating Royalist cavalry as far as two miles from Leicester, which was twenty miles away. 'The horse', observed Belasyse caustically, 'knew well how to save themselves, tho' not their honours, by a hasty and shameful flight to Leicester, without staying to bring off His Majesty, who at last (with the best of his officers and his own guards) retired and found all those shattered horse under the walls of Leicester.'[15] The Parliamentarian infantry captured the Royalist baggage train, which they plundered, and also killed 100 women and soldiers' wives, 'some of quality', hiding there. Others had their faces slashed and their noses slit, on the ground that they were whores or Irish papists, though most of them were no doubt Welsh.

The number of soldiers killed in the battle was remarkably few. According to the commissioners from Parliament who were observers with the New Model Army and reported to the Speaker of the House of Commons, 600 Royalist soldiers were killed and 200 Roundheads. Colonel Okey stated that he did not lose 'a single man' in his regiment of dragoons.[16] From the Royalist side Walker asserted that 'not 200 lost their lives in the battle'; Belasyse said the same.[17] King Charles and Prince Rupert were silent about their defeat except that Rupert knew he would be blamed for it and threatened 'to quit generalship'. Unquestionably 5,000 prisoners were taken – 4,500 private soldiers and 500 officers. It also appears that some 200 cavalrymen were captured: '200 horse with their riders' is what Sprigge wrote, which was magnified into 'two thousand horse with their Riders taken' in the unreliable pamphlet entitled *A True Relation*. According to Sir Thomas Fairfax, 'the whole body of the foot' were 'taken or slain'.[18] In addition the Royalists lost their whole train of artillery and 8,000 arms.

A serious consequence of the battle of Naseby for Charles was that a cabinet of the King's private papers was discovered on the field and sent up to Westminster by General Fairfax. These included drafts or copies of letters written by the King to his wife in France. Charles laughed off the publication of the letters as best he could, but they were of enormous propaganda value to the victors and severely damaged the Royalist cause.

General Fairfax recorded the 'never to be forgotten mercy' which God had given them. Lieutenant-General Cromwell in a famous letter to the Speaker of the House of Commons, after stating that to God 'alone belongs the glory', thought fit as a member of parliament to commend the Commander-in-Chief for his 'faithfulness and honour', and concluded:

> Honest men served you in this action. Sir, they are trusty. I beseech you in the name of God not to discourage them. I wish the action may beget thankfulness and humility in all that are concerned in it. He that ventures his life for the liberty of his country I wish he trust God for the liberty of his conscience and you for the liberty he fights for.[19]

The last paragraph of his letter was omitted by the House of Commons when it was published: many of its members did not for one moment think that the war was being fought to preserve liberty of conscience, rather the contrary. It is one of the aspects of the greatness of Oliver Cromwell, who was, in fact, the principal architect of the victory of Naseby, that this was one of his own profound beliefs.

8 The Battle of Naseby – III

Why was the battle of Naseby fought at all? At the beginning of the civil war it was hoped by both sides that its result would be determined by a single battle. But single battles have not generally won wars. 'Battles', noted Michael Roberts, at this stage in European history 'became . . . justified (if at all) as clearing the way for further operations . . . [as a] strategy aimed at the occupation of territory rather than annihilation.'[1] Most generals were convinced in the early part of the seventeenth century, including, for example, Prince Maurice of Orange, that sieges were more valuable than battles. The capture of a stronghold was then believed to be a vital gain, whereas a battle was always a gamble.

To a large extent this military philosophy coloured the first civil war after the Royalists' partial victory at Edgehill and their failure to conquer London. In 1644, so long as Taunton and Plymouth remained under the control of Parliamentarian garrisons, King Charles's victory at the battle of Lostwithiel had not secured the south-west of England to the Royalists, while the capture of Bristol by Prince Rupert in 1643 had done much to ensure Cavalier supremacy in the west. It was in an effort to complete this supremacy that the King had vainly tried to take Gloucester by siege. On the other hand, in the north of England, so long as the city of Chester remained uncaptured by the Parliamentarians and the Scots failed to subdue Pontefract Castle in the centre of Yorkshire, the victory won by Cromwell's troops at Marston Moor with the aid of the Scottish army had not guaranteed Parliament's complete hold there.

One of King Charles's chief concerns at the outset of the campaign of 1645 had been to relieve Chester from its siege by Sir William Brereton; Prince Rupert also wanted to do so and afterwards to march on to the relief of Pontefract Castle. For its part the Committee of Both Kingdoms had been eager first to relieve Taunton and then to occupy Oxford. When Fairfax was preparing to besiege Oxford Charles retorted by assaulting Leicester after dispatching Goring to resume the siege of Taunton. So it was not until the Committee of Both Kingdoms started worrying about the safety of East Anglia, which apart from London itself was the only area the Parliamentarians had dominated throughout the war, and therefore gave Fairfax and his New Model Army a free hand to take the offensive against the King, following his capture of Leicester, that the likelihood of a battle between the two sides again arose.[2]

When Charles was settled in Daventry he contemplated the possibility of a battle without dismay. His civilian advisers, such as Lord Culpeper, who wrote from Bath that he felt certain that the 'new raw army' could not take Oxford, and Lord Digby, who was convinced that if Major-General Goring returned from the west they could surprise the rebels with an unexpected advantage of superiority, persuaded Charles, as he wrote to his wife, that the future was bright and a battle not to be feared.[3]

It has invariably been a mistake in warfare to underestimate one's enemy. Prince Rupert was fully aware that until the King's army was reinforced it was dangerous to risk a battle and wiser to rest on the laurels gained at Leicester. As has been noted, most of the officers at the Council of War, as distinct from the civilians, were against doing so, but Charles was induced to believe that he had no need to shrink from facing Fairfax's untried army. So the battle was not really forced upon him. For it is, in fact, likely that, had the decision been taken when Charles left Daventry to move away north, he could have succeeded in moving out of the reach of the New Model Army.

Plainly General Fairfax himself thought that the King might have withdrawn safely from Market Harborough to Leicester had he wished to do so. Nevertheless, when the King's Council of War met at midnight on 13 June, the resolution was taken – contrary to Prince Rupert's advice – to 'move back' from Market Harborough and 'seek out' the enemy rather than 'to be sought and pursued'. Thus, if one accepts the accuracy of Sprigge's conclusion from his examination of the evidence that it was 'the King's counsel' that 'prevailed against the mind of most of his great officers',[4] it is Charles I who must bear the responsibility for the battle being fought at all because he allowed himself to be convinced that the New Model Army was raw and untried and that it might prove to be an easy prey.

Once the Royalists elected to fight, however, it was Prince Rupert who directed the tactics. Had the Royalist army remained deployed on its original position along the ridge running through Little Oxendon and north of East Farndon, a position which, as Colonel Rogers noted, was 'well suited for defence by a smaller force',[5] it might have won a defensive battle if Fairfax had attacked it there. But when Rupert undertook his own reconnaissance of the Parliamentarian lines along the hills north-west of Naseby village he wrongly came to the conclusion that he would be able to surprise his enemy – the idea that he was confident it was retreating can surely be discounted – and therefore persuaded the King to redeploy his army on Dust Hill, where the slope was more gentle than that from the East Farndon ridge. Sir Edward Walker wrote: 'this made us quit our Ground of Advantage and in reasonable order to advance'.[6]

Still, once Rupert had made up his mind to attack in the hope of achieving surprise, it was logical for him to move the whole army forward and lead it over Broad Moor from Dust Hill. That the surprise was effective is proved by the account given by Colonel Okey when he wrote:

> So soon as we came into the field the Enemy was drawn up into a Battalia ready to give us battle . . . they were ready to advance upon us before we were all drawn up into a Battalia for to encounter them.[7]

They were, he added, 'thinking to daunt us, or at least to take us before we were ready to give them entertainment . . .' and whatever Walker thought about 'quitting our ground of advantage', he admitted that Prince Rupert 'with his own and Prince Maurice's troops . . . did so well and were so well seconded that they bore all down before them'.[8] Up to that point Rupert's tactics were successful.

If a strong case can be made out for Rupert undertaking an offensive in an effort to surprise the Parliamentarian left wing, the difficulty is to justify his action, after he had defeated Colonel Butler's regiment, in pushing on to capture the large Parliamentarian baggage train established near Naseby village. He had committed the same mistake at the battle of Edgehill, but there the baggage train at Kineton was surrounded on both flanks and the bulk of the Parliamentarian cavalry had been overrun except for two regiments. At Naseby the result of Rupert's departure from the main battleground was not only to leave the infantry 'naked' but to allow Commissary-General Ireton the time and opportunity to redeploy his forces; and meanwhile on his left wing Cromwell was able to overpower the relatively small Royalist cavalry contingent which had been ordered to take the offensive against him and then to turn his attention to attacking the Royalist infantrymen who had been fighting so bravely in the centre.

Even if Rupert had not been defied by the firelocks and musketeers guarding the baggage train, his troopers would undoubtedly have given themselves over to plunder and thus have made it harder for the Prince to induce his men to return to the fighting on the main battlefield. As Brigadier Young pointed out:

> It seems extraordinary that a man of Rupert's intelligence with the lessons of Edgehill engraved on his heart should have wasted time in this fashion. If he won the battle the train would be his for the taking.[9]

The Retreat at Naseby, *a mezzotint by W. Giller from a painting by Abraham Cooper, mid-nineteenth century*

In fact, when General Fairfax won the battle the Royalists lost their entire baggage train.

It occupied an hour for Rupert to bring back his men; by then they were so tired and demoralized that they could not be induced 'to rally themselves again in order to charge the enemy'. As the Earl of Clarendon wrote in his *History of the Rebellion*:

> . . . the difference in the discipline of the King's troops and those which marched under the command of Cromwell [was] that though the King's troops prevailed in the charge [as Rupert did at Naseby] and routed those they charged, they never rallied themselves again in order, nor to make a second charge again the same day.[10]

The Prince was therefore fully aware that he would be condemned for the defeat, and several leading Royalists, such as Clarendon, Sir Richard Bulstrode and by implication Sir Edward Walker, all did so.

Nevertheless, Charles deserves to bear most of the blame. In the first place he overruled Rupert's advice to avoid fighting the battle at all. He had also delayed so long in Daventry that he allowed Fairfax ample time to catch up with his army and endanger its withdrawal north. Secondly, Charles ought to have recognized by this stage in the civil war what an impetuous general his nephew was. In that case he should have ordered Prince Maurice to take charge on the right wing of the battle line and kept Rupert with him to supervise the progress of the battle in the same way as General Fairfax was able to do on the other side. If he had then thrown in his reserve at the right time in support of Sir Marmaduke Langdale – though admittedly it might not have determined the result of the battle – at least it might have prevented Cromwell from attacking the infantry. As it was, when Charles attempted to employ his reserve, it proved to be too late to transform the situation. Instead complete confusion developed so that in the end both Charles and Rupert were compelled to take flight with the remnants of their cavalry as far as Leicester.

One may conclude that the Royalists did not lose the battle of Naseby, as is generally contended, because they were vastly outnumbered by the Parliamentarians, for to some extent quality compensated for quantity. The Royalist infantrymen were superior to their enemy and fought effectively until they were assaulted on both flanks by cavalry and dragoons. Then, as experienced soldiers, they realized that their situation was hopeless and surrendered in droves. Rupert concentrated the best of his cavalry on the right wing, where, as an officer on the other side wrote, 'the King's horse routed us clear beyond our carriages'.[11] Moreover, Sir Marmaduke Langdale's Yorkshiremen, who were said to have obeyed him as the Roman centurions obeyed Julius Caesar, supported by the horse from the Newark, also fought courageously, while Sir Marmaduke even offered to assist Prince Rupert by making one last charge. Sir Edward Walker considered that 'had our left Wing but done half so well as either the Foot or the right Wing' at the outset of the battle 'we had got in a few minutes a glorious victory'.[12]

What most emphatically differentiated the two armies was the quality of the generalship. Sir Thomas Fairfax may be said to have belonged to a family of soldiers. His grandfather had shared camp life with Sir Horace Vere in the Netherlands; two of his uncles were killed fighting in the Palatinate; he had, after being educated in Cambridge, served Vere and married his daughter Anne. He acquired further military experience as a cavalry officer in Charles I's abortive wars against the Scottish Covenanters. Once the civil war began he distinguished himself as a commander in the West Riding of Yorkshire and in the defence of Hull and was victorious at the battles of Winceby in East Anglia, Nantwich in Cheshire and Selby in North Yorkshire. Thus he was the best-qualified general in the service of Parliament. Sprigge wrote of him:

When he hath come upon action, or been near an engagement it hath been observed, another spirit hath come upon him, another soul hath looked out at his eyes; I mean, he hath been so raised, elevated, and transported, as that he hath been not only unlike himself at other times, but indeed more like an angel than a man.[13]

At Naseby he demonstrated that a Commander-in-Chief could overcome the difficulties of taking full control in a major battle. First, he drew up the bulk of his cavalry in the hills before the village; then he deployed the infantry with the help of Major-General Skippon. Once the battle opened it was said: 'His Excellency the General was everywhere the occasion required it.' Initially mounted on his chestnut mare he was with Cromwell on the right wing, but as soon as he perceived that his infantry was in danger he returned with his Lifeguard and brought forward the second or reserve line of foot. Finally he organized a combined attack of cavalry and infantry which broke the resistance of Sir George Lisle's gallant brigade on the Royalist right centre. As his biographer, Clements Markham, wrote: 'he was on the spot wherever his presence was needed' and always kept a cool head.[14]

An obelisk built in the reign of Queen Victoria to commemorate the battle of Naseby. It is situated where there was a mill to the east of the village of Naseby, not on the actual site of the battlefield

If Fairfax was an extremely capable commander-in-chief, Oliver Cromwell was a military genius. He was not victorious, as has been claimed, simply because he was on the side of the big battalions. Anyone who has studied his victories at Preston in 1648 and Dunbar in 1650 can recognize the absurdity of that argument. It was he who won the battle of Marston Moor after Fairfax had been defeated on the right wing. At Naseby Fairfax had accepted his advice about the deployment of the troops before Naseby village while it was his swift defeat of Langdale that enabled Fairfax to overwhelm the Royalist infantry compelling them to face surrender rather than die with their boots on. Although it is an exaggeration to say that Cromwell never suffered a setback in his military career – he was twice outwitted by Goring in the 1645 campaign and was to endure severe losses when he laid siege to Clonmel in Ireland in 1649 – attempts by modern military historians to denigrate the parts he played in the victories at Marston Moor and Dunbar have no substance whatever. Nor does the fact that he never fought outside the British Isles detract from his military genius. 'His great strength', Professor Austin Woolrych has recently observed:

> . . . lay in his ability to raise and train cavalry regiments of superb courage and discipline, to fire them with his own high sense that they were fighting the Lord's battles, and to lead them in the field with a keen eye that told him where their striking power was most needed and would be most effective.[15]

That was fully exemplified at Naseby. To sum up, it was generalship, not superior numbers or better equipment, that accounts for the Parliamentarian triumph at the battle of Naseby.

9 The Aftermath of Naseby

General Fairfax did not pursue the King's remaining troopers all the way to Leicester, but gave orders for his entire army 'to march after them next day, which', in Joshua Sprigge's words, 'was the Lord's Day'. The soldiers obeyed him cheerfully even though they might have 'pleaded for some time for refreshment'. By then the New Model cavalry was within a mile of Leicester and on the following day the town was surrounded; yet it was not until 18 June that the Governor, Lord Loughborough, surrendered on honourable terms. Charles had not lingered in Leicester, but led his surviving cavalry, numbering some 4,000, north-west to Ashby-de-la-Zouch; then he turned south-west through Lichfield and Wolverhampton and reached the small town of Bewdley in Herefordshire on 18 June. Here he and Prince Rupert made the best of their misfortunes, counting on being able to build up a new army mainly from Welshmen and Irishmen. Rupert wrote about this to William Legge, the Governor of Oxford, noting that Sir Charles Gerard, who, having fought successfully for the King in South Wales, was still in command of 4,000 infantrymen and 1,000 cavalrymen in the Hereford area: 'so, I hope, in a short time we shall be stronger than ever'.[2] On the same day the King wrote to the Marquis of Ormonde, his Lord Lieutenant in Ireland:

> The late misfortune which I have had makes the Irish assistance more necessary than before; and now the speedy performance of it is almost of as great importance as the thing itself; the which I must earnestly recommend to your wonted care and diligence. For if within these two months you could send me a considerable assistance, I am confident that both my last loss would be soon forgotten, and likewise it may (by the Grace of God) put such a turn to my affairs as to make me in a far better condition before winter than I have been at any time since the rebellion began.[3]

But Ormonde, a Protestant, had never been anxious to recruit Irish Catholics to fight for the King in England; and for that reason earlier in the year Charles had dispatched Edward Somerset, Earl of Glamorgan, heir to the wealthy Marquis of Worcester, who was a Roman Catholic, with instructions to enlist

10,000 Irishmen to fight for him in return for a promise that he would ultimately repeal the recusancy laws which punished those who did not attend Anglican services. Although Glamorgan had been told to act in consultation with Ormonde, the Lord Lieutenant was offended by his mission, even though Glamorgan had been instructed by Charles to offer him the award of a Garter as a consolation prize. When Charles arrived at Hereford on 23 June he wrote to Glamorgan to tell him that he was 'no wise disheartened by our late Misfortune' and that he hoped to recover our 'late loss with advantage if he received succour from the kingdom of Ireland'.[4] But Glamorgan exceeded his instructions and in the end nothing came of his intervention.

One of the most serious consequences of the defeat at Naseby for King Charles was over the packet of his private letters and papers that were captured on the battlefield. Since they were written in his own handwriting to his wife in France their authenticity could not be denied and they were at once printed and circulated as Parliamentarian propaganda. Stress was laid on an offer to grant 'a toleration of Idolatry to Papists' and an 'indemnity to the murderous Irish' in return for the military assistance sought by Glamorgan. In one letter he had written to the Queen: 'I give thee power to promise in my name (to whom thou thinkest most fit) that I will take away all the penal laws against Roman Catholics in England.' Furthermore these letters revealed that he was trying to hire an army of French mercenaries commanded by the Duke of Lorraine to be carried to England by Dutch transport vessels through the agency of his son-in-law, Prince William of Orange. The letters were edited and published in a pamphlet entitled *The King's Cabinet Opened* and their authenticity emphasized; a foreword concluded: 'God grant that the drawing of the curtain may be fatal to Popery and all Anti-Christian heresy here now, as the rending of the veil was to the Jewish ceremonies in Judea at the expiration of our Saviour.' The King also lost the manuscript of a book he had started to write as an apologia for his own policies before the civil war began. This was, in fact, to be restored to him when he was later the prisoner of the Parliamentary army at Hampton Court in 1647 and formed part of the book called *Eikon Basilike* which was published after his execution in 1649.

Prince Rupert left the King in Hereford, crossed the river Severn and after visiting the Prince of Wales, who was in Barnstaple, took over command in Bristol, from where the Prince of Wales and his advisers had withdrawn. Rupert was still disgruntled at being blamed for the defeat at Naseby: he confided to his friend, William Legge, that he had received more kindness from Prince Charles, who was in nominal command in the west of England, than he had done from his father. The King went on from Hereford to Abergavenny in South Wales and thence to the splendid fortified palace of the aged Marquis of Worcester at

Raglan, which he reached on 3 July, having covered a distance of some 150 miles since his retreat from Naseby. He stayed at Raglan for four weeks: he played bowls, inspected the ingenious waterworks erected there and went to church. Sir Edward Walker, who was with him wrote: 'We were there all lulled asleep with Sports and Entertainments.' Hence Charles wrote optimistically: 'I have such good hope of my Welsh levies that I doubt not (by the Grace of God) to be at the head of the greatest army within two months that I have seen this year.'[5]

Lord Digby, his Secretary of State, who was also with him, had already noted that Charles was 'no wise disheartened by our late Misfortune', counting on help from Ireland as well as from Wales.[6]

Charles's confidence, however, lacked foundation. It was based on a variety of considerations, none of which had any substance at all. He believed that with the valuable city of Bristol still in Royalist hands, as well as the fortress of Bridgwater in Somerset, and with General Goring possessing an army of 7,000 men still besieging Taunton, his hold on the west of England was strong; he knew that the Marquis of Montrose was winning victories for him in Scotland; he relied on recruiting reinforcements in Wales and Ireland; and he even counted on his wife raising the army of mercenaries in France which could be landed in Kent, where he contemplated going to meet them. His problem, as he meditated about his future amid the comforts of Raglan Castle, was what should he best do next. Should he make for Scotland? Should he ensure the safety of Chester, where reinforcements from Ireland could be landed? Should he join Goring in the west of England? Charles seriously examined the last course, which arguably would have been the wisest, as the Earl of Clarendon noted in his *History of the Rebellion*, for the King might then have been able to concentrate an army of as many as 15,000 trained soldiers, a force capable of countering the victorious New Model Army.

However, while Charles was still at Raglan he learned first that Lieutenant-General Goring had been defeated at the battle of Langport in Somerset on 10 July and later that Bridgwater had been captured by General Fairfax, who had led his army into the west of England soon after his victory at Naseby. Although Charles held a conference with Prince Rupert at Crick, near Chepstow in Wales, on 21 July, where they agreed that he should embark upon a campaign in the west, taking up his headquarters at Bristol, yet once he learned of the fate of Bridgwater he changed his mind and determined instead to start out on a secret journey to link up with the Marquis of Montrose, who was still triumphant in Scotland. When Rupert heard of this change of plan he thought it was 'a strange decision' and informed his friend, the 1st Duke of Richmond, who was one of the King's courtiers and had married the daughter of the 1st Duke of Buckingham: 'His Majesty hath now no way left to preserve his posterity,

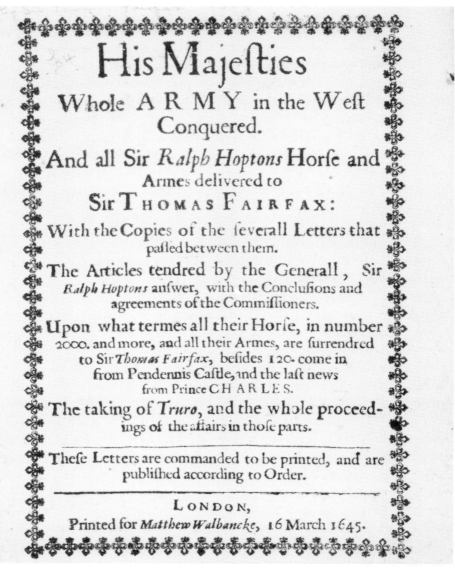

His Majesties

Whole ARMY in the West Conquered.

And all Sir *Ralph Hoptons* Horse and Armes delivered to

Sir THOMAS FAIRFAX:

With the Copies of the severall Letters that passed between them.

The Articles tendred by the Generall, Sir *Ralph Hoptons* answer, with the Conclusions and agreements of the Commissioners.

Upon what termes all their Horse, in number 2000. and more, and all their Armes, are surrendred to Sir *Thomas Fairfax*, besides 120. come in from Pendennis Castle, and the last news from Prince CHARLES.

The taking of *Truro*, and the whole proceedings of the affairs in those parts.

These Letters are commanded to be printed, and are published according to Order.

LONDON,
Printed for *Matthew Walbancke*, 16 March 1645.

After Charles lost the battle of Naseby General Fairfax, who defeated him, marched into the west of England and beat the Royalist army under General Goring at Langport in Somerset on 10 July 1645. After that he overwhelmed the remaining Royalist forces in the west, commanded by Lord Hopton, who capitulated completely in March 1646. The illustration shows the title page of the terms of the surrender printed in London

kingdom and nobility but by a treaty . . . a more prudent way to obtain something than to lose all.'[7] When the Duke showed Rupert's letter to the King, Charles wrote to him from Cardiff: 'I confess, that, speaking as a mere soldier or statesman, I must say there is no probability but of my ruin', but insisted that he trusted to God 'not to suffer rebels or traitors to prosper' and declared he must fight on.[8] Two days later Charles wrote to his eldest son telling him that it was 'very fit to prepare for the worst' and that if he was in danger of falling into the hands of the rebels he should go to France and stay with his mother.[9] Then with a contingent of 2,200 cavalry and 400 infantry he crossed the Welsh mountains, passed through Shropshire, Staffordshire and Derbyshire to arrive on 18 August at Doncaster in Yorkshire, where he believed his condition was 'miraculously good' because he was joined by a group of volunteers;[10] but, being confronted by two enemy forces, he retired south to plunder Huntingdon, Oliver Cromwell's birthplace, and finally returned to Oxford on 28 August.

Two days later the indefatigable King was off again. He had been cheered at Huntingdon with the news of another victory by Montrose over a superior Covenanter army at Kilsyth, north of Glasgow. But he was by this time resolved that it was impossible for him to find his own way to Scotland and instead his thoughts turned back again to the west of England.

In September Charles enjoyed his last military success in the first civil war. Montrose's victories in southern Scotland had induced General David Leslie, who had come south to besiege the key town of Hereford, to abandon its siege and send the cavalry back north so that the King, with the support of additional cavalry summoned from Oxford, was able to reoccupy the town unopposed. But he was deeply concerned about the security of Bristol because General Fairfax, after his victory at Langport and capture of Bridgwater, had arrived there at the head of an army numbering some 10,000 men. Prince Rupert had assured the King that he could hold the city for four months. There were ample provisions available so that a siege might easily have been withstood. Yet its garrison consisted of a mere 1,500 men and the circuit round the walls measured five miles. After Rupert had organized six sallies against the besiegers Fairfax ordered that it should be stormed and a fierce bombardment was launched on all sides of the city. The assault from the south was contained, but on the north and east the Roundheads surged across the walls, threatening the inner defences and the citadel. At five o'clock in the morning of 8 September Rupert judged that the situation was hopeless and after consulting his Council of War surrendered on generous terms.

King Charles, now back in Raglan Castle, was furious when he learned of the surrender ten days after he had raised the siege of Hereford. He had planned to relieve Bristol himself with the help of Goring, whom he had summoned from

A
SERMON
PREACHED

Before the Honourable House
OF
COMMONS

At WESTMINSTER,
August 22. 1645.

Being the day appointed for their Solemn
Thankſgiving unto God for his ſeveral Mercies
to the Forces of the Parliament in divers
parts of the Kingdome,

In the Gaining of the Towns of *Bath* and
Bridgewater, and of *Scarborough*-Caſtle, and
Sherborn-Caſtle, and for the diſperſing
of the Clubmen, and the good
Succeſſe in *Pembroke*-ſhire.

By *Thomas Caſe*, Preacher at *Milkſtreet*, and one
of the Aſſembly of Divines.

LONDON,
Printed by *Ruth Raworth*, for *Luke Fawne*, at the ſigne of
the *Parrot* in *Pauls* Church-yard. 1645.

A sermon of thanksgiving for the taking of Bath and Bridgwater by the Parliamentarian forces, 1645

the west. But Rupert did not know of this. Clements Markham, Fairfax's biographer, was of the opinion that Rupert 'might undoubtedly have held out for a considerable time longer' and that it was political and not military reasons that persuaded him to surrender so easily.[11] Charles thought that the Prince could have withdrawn his forces into the citadel and awaited relief. But even if Goring had come to the rescue it would have been three weeks before he arrived. Once Fairfax decided to storm the city it was, in fact, doomed. Unquestionably, Rupert was weary of the war and disgusted over his treatment by his uncle, who had more than once, usually at the prompting of Lord Digby, overruled his advice. That Charles may have been suspicious that Rupert was hoping that his elder brother, the Elector Palatine, who was in the good books of the Parliamentarians, might replace his uncle on the throne of England, as has been suggested, seems highly unlikely.[12] Eventually, during October, when the King was at Newark, Rupert and his brother Maurice forced their way into his presence, a Council of War examined the evidence about the loss of Bristol, and afterwards Charles declared that Rupert had not been guilty of any want of courage or infidelity to his service, but implied that he had been indiscreet. Furthermore, he indignantly repudiated Rupert's claim that he was a child taking orders from Lord Digby – only 'rogues and rascals' would say so. So Rupert was not restored to his offices and during the summer of 1646, in answer to his own request, he and his brother were allowed to leave England for France.

Before then, during the autumn of 1645, two further disasters confronted the King. First, although still intending to march north to join Montrose, he decided to try to relieve Chester, which was still under siege by the Parliamentarians, and was important to him because he continued to hope to welcome reinforcements

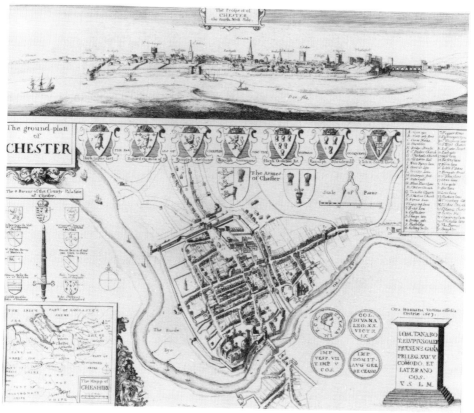

A sketch and plan of the city of Chester, 1653, engraved by Hollar

landing there from Ireland. On 23 September he managed to enter Chester on the Welsh side with his Lifeguards, and while he remained in the city with the infantry he ordered a sortie by the cavalry under the command of Sir Marmaduke Langdale, the austere, aristocratic figure known as 'the ghost', who had escaped from Naseby. The idea was that Langdale should cross the river Dee to the south of Chester in order to attack the enemy from the rear. But the besiegers were reinforced by Colonel-General Sydenham Poyntz, who had replaced Lord Fairfax in command of the Yorkshire Parliamentarians, and he overpowered and defeated Langdale in what became known as the battle of Rowton Moor, eight miles to the south-east of the city. Thus Charles lost 1,000 men dead or prisoners and was obliged to retreat into Wales. Here (at Denbigh) Charles learned a few days later of his other setback: Montrose's small army had at last been surrounded, outnumbered and massacred by a Covenanter army at Philiphaugh near Melrose in southern Scotland on 13 September. Charles then wrote that his loss at Rowton Moor and the false news he had received that Montrose had been killed at Philiphaugh 'put me into a fit of deep melancholy and despair that I have never been subject unto'.[13]

A week later Charles arrived at Newark, one of the very few towns in England still held by the Royalists, with the remnants of his army. Here, after he had dealt with Rupert, as related above, he again contemplated making for Scotland, but first galloped back to Oxford, where he arrived exhausted at ten o'clock on the night of 5 November. Thence he despatched his favourite, Lord Digby, whom he had appointed Lieutenant-General, to go north instead of himself with a few hundred troopers to try to find Montrose, as he now knew that the Marquis had escaped uninjured after his defeat. In Oxford Charles's stern treatment of Rupert and continued reliance on Digby caused demoralization in his small, over-officered army. Clarendon wrote:

> And so, he finished the most tedious and grievous march that ever king was exercised in, having been almost in perpetual motion from the loss of the battle of Naseby to this hour, with such variety of dismal accidents as must have broken the spirits of any man who had not been the most magnanimous person in the world.[14]

10 The End of the First Civil War

King Charles's military position was now hopeless. In western England General Goring, after his defeat at Langport, followed by a prolonged period of idleness and debauchery at Exeter, departed from the country altogether during November.

The Prince of Wales's Council appointed Lord Hopton, one of the most able Royalist commanders, in his place, but he had a force of no more than 5,000 men at his disposal. In Worcester the veteran infantry officer, Lord Astley, who had survived the defeat at Naseby, collected some 3,000 men, while at Chester the remains of the garrison under Lord Byron, even after the losses on Rowton Moor, had been reinforced by a few troops from Wales. Charles told his wife that he had 2,000 foot and horse available in his smaller garrisons.

These scattered contingents were of little value. The King's only prospect of substantial reinforcements were the 7,000 mercenaries he counted on the Queen being able to hire in France and the 10,000 Confederate Irish soldiers that the Earl of Glamorgan had been trying to recruit for him in return for lavish promises of religious concessions, intending to send them by sea to Chester. None of these schemes came to anything at all. Glamorgan's secret negotiations became public knowledge; Charles was therefore obliged to repudiate him and the Marquis of Ormonde arrested and imprisoned him. Moreover, on 3 February 1646 Lord Byron surrendered Chester, which had at last been starved out by the besiegers. A fortnight later Fairfax overwhelmed Hopton at the battle of Torrington in north Devon. The Prince of Wales, realizing that the war in the west of England was now lost by the Royalists, therefore fled from Cornwall to the Scilly Islands where his chief counsellor, Sir Edward Hyde, the future Earl of Clarendon, began writing his celebrated *History of the Rebellion*. Finally Lord Astley, who had been ordered by the King to join him in Oxford, was defeated by Sydenham Poyntz on his way there at Stow-on-the-Wold on 20 March. That was the last field army. Thus the fitful gleams of satisfaction from military events or hopes for the recruitment of reinforcements that shone on the King faded between the time he escaped from Naseby and when he settled back in Oxford during the winter of 1645–6.

Having then nothing of military value left with which to do battle other than his garrisons in Oxford, Newark and parts of Wales and Cornwall, and vague promises of recruits from Ireland and France, Charles was driven to seek, as Prince Rupert had advised him to do, for the best terms he could obtain from the victorious Parliamentarians by diplomatic means. A month after his return to Oxford he wrote to the House of Lords proposing to send a delegation to Westminster to open negotiations for peace. When that was refused by both Houses of Parliament he wrote on Boxing Day offering to come to London himself:

> . . . to enter into a personal treaty with the two Houses of Parliament at Westminster and the commissioners of the Parliament of Scotland upon all matters which might conduce to the peace and happiness of the distracted kingdoms.

Queen Henriette Marie was extremely disturbed at the idea of her husband's going to London and thus putting himself into the power of the rebels. Charles assured her that he would be in no danger whatsoever so long as the Prince of Wales and the Duke of York were out of their reach;[1] he also relied for the success of such a mission upon the known divisions between the Presbyterians and Independents in the House of Commons, hoping that one or the other would 'side with him . . . so that I shall really be a king again'. 'If I cannot be a king,' he told Lord Digby, 'I shall die like a gentleman.'[2]

The Queen, however, pressed him to give way to the Presbyterians in their demands while he stuck to the view that completely to abandon the episcopacy would be 'a sin of the highest nature'.[3] The most he would offer was to tolerate Presbyterianism after the episcopal Church of England was re-established. However, as it became known in London that Charles had allowed negotiations to be resumed with the Confederate Roman Catholic leaders in Ireland, to whom promises of the full recognition of the rights of their Church in dependence upon the Papacy were given, this cut little ice. Indeed, it was also learnt in London in January 1646 that the Queen had sent an emissary, the Roman Catholic Sir Kenelm Digby, to beg help for her husband from Pope Innocent I in return for the abolition of penal statutes against the Roman Catholics in England as well as in Ireland. The Parliamentarians – anti-papist to a man – were infuriated and the two Houses firmly rejected Charles's repeated requests to return to Westminster to discuss the terms on which he would be allowed to step back on to his throne.

While Charles had been vainly trying to negotiate with the English Parliament since his defeat at Naseby, he also had another scheme up his sleeve: this was to

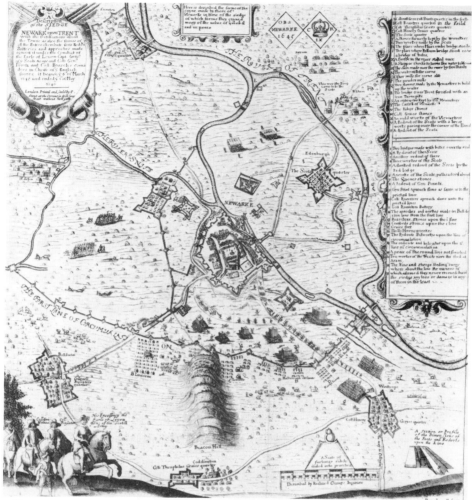

Newark-on-Trent in Nottinghamshire, the important strategic town held by the Royalists throughout the first civil war. It was relieved by Prince Rupert after a siege by the Parliamentarians in 1644, but was under siege once more from March 1645 to May 1646, when the garrison finally surrendered at the command of King Charles

invoke the support of the Scottish Covenanter leaders, who still had an army stationed in England engaged in besieging Newark. He was inspired in this idea by the arrival in England of a young French diplomatist named Jean de Montreuil, who had been ordered there by Cardinal Mazarin, the effective ruler of France, with the specific task of mediating between Charles and the Scots. The Scottish Covenanters were determined that they would help Charles only if he agreed to make Presbyterianism, instead of episcopacy, the State religion of

England. Montreuil was at first optimistic. 'The King,' he said, 'ought to prefer the preservation of his Crown to that of all the mitres in the country'.[4]

Montreuil arrived in England in July 1645, about six weeks after the battle of Naseby, but it was not until April 1646 that he succeeded in persuading Charles to put himself into the hands of the Scottish army stationed near Newark, where (Montreuil said) he would be received as a sovereign, treated honourably, and given the opportunity to procure their assistance in obtaining a happy peace. The Scots, however, took it for granted that in return for their active help the King would consent to the strict imposition of Presbyterianism as the national religion in England, as it already was in Scotland, while Charles for his part failed to credit the belief that the Scots would insist upon that commitment as the price for aiding him to regain his throne. So a misunderstanding developed between the two sides when on 6 April 1646 Charles wrote to his wife to assure her that Montreuil had arranged that he would be received into the Scottish army 'as their natural sovereign with freedom of my conscience and honour and all my servants and followers are to be safely and honourably protected'.[5]

During the next fortnight Charles was extremely perplexed about his future. For whatever promises the Scottish commissioners in London might have given to Montreuil about how he would be received if he arrived at the Scottish army headquarters near Newark, now under the command of General David Leslie, it turned out that the commissioners there had no intention whatever of welcoming the King officially or giving him any guarantees about what they would do for him if he came to meet them. Realizing this, Montreuil now changed his mind and attempted to persuade Charles not to join the Scottish army. Prince Rupert, who had at last been formally reconciled to his uncle and had returned to Oxford, also strongly advised the King not to do so, though when Charles insisted on going he volunteered to accompany him. At first Charles contemplated taking both Rupert and Maurice with him when he departed from Oxford, but he rejected the idea because he felt that if they went in disguise Rupert would 'be discovered because of his tallness'. Having finally made up his mind to leave Oxford at the end of April he still had not yet decided, as he told his wife a few days before he went, whether he would try 'to procure honourable and safe conditions from the rebels, sail to Scotland, Ireland, France or Denmark'.[6] In fact, he did none of these things. He removed from his quarters in Oxford disguised as a servant, accompanied by his friend and courtier, John Ashburnham, and by one of his chaplains, Michael Hudson, crossed Magdalen Bridge at three o'clock on the morning of 27 April, and set out for Hillingdon in Middlesex where he waited for three hours, evidently expecting an emissary from the capital city, possibly the Lord Mayor of London, to meet him there. No one arrived, and after a circuitous journey lasting ten days, he eventually reached

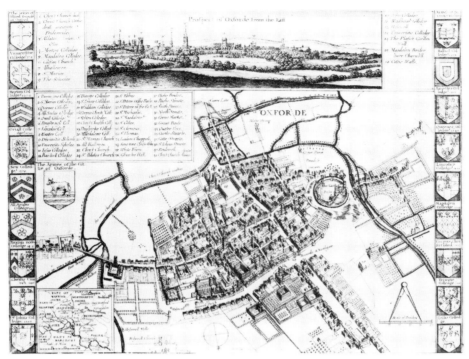

A contemporary Prospect of Oxforde from the East *and map of Oxford by Hollar. The badges on the sides are those of the colleges*

the Scottish military headquarters outside Newark. Here he was treated as a prisoner and compelled to order the Royalist garrison of Newark to surrender to the English Parliamentarian force under Sydenham Poyntz which was also encamped outside the town. Actually, according to Clarendon's *History*, the King was anxious for the Scottish army to leave the Newark area as soon as possible and move off north so that it would be out of the reach of General Fairfax and the main Parliamentarian army which, he feared, might be ordered to leave the siege of Oxford where it was then engaged, in order to seize him as their prisoner.

The Queen had long been pressing her husband to join the Scots because she hoped that if he would agree to accept an omnipotent Presbyterian Church in England, as they wanted him to do, they in return would ensure his return to the throne. Although he had received no undertakings of any kind either directly from Montreuil or through Hudson, whom he had sent to contact Montreuil in early May, he felt confident that he would 'eschew all kind of captivity' once he escaped from Oxford, which he recognized was doomed and soon to surrender to the Parliamentarians. In fact, the Scots, who maintained that they were surprised by his arrival at their camp, did make him captive and denied that they had ever promised to enter into negotiations about his future with him. So he found himself suffering the most 'barbarous usage' he had ever experienced in his life. He was allowed neither personal servants nor chaplains. Ashburnham was obliged to leave him for fear he would be put under arrest and sent to London. Charles soon realized, as he was to tell the Queen: 'the Scots will absolutely hinder my being any more King in England than they have made me in Scotland'.[7]

After they left Newark the Scottish army carried the King off to Newcastle upon Tyne. Here Charles sent his permission to the Governor of Oxford to treat for its surrender to General Fairfax. He did so reluctantly. The terms meant that Prince Rupert was allowed to go abroad, but the King's second son, James, Duke of York, who was still in the city, became a prisoner of the Parliament-arians. The governors of such other Royalist garrisons as were intact were also ordered to surrender and the Marquis of Montrose was instructed by the King to disband such troops as he still had with him in Scotland and find exile in France. Thus, a year after the disaster at Naseby King Charles's Scottish captors

Charles I and his second son, James, Duke of York, painted by Sir Peter Lely, c. 1647

explained to him that 'when His Majesty had no more forts or foot nor garrisons which held out for him, it could not be denied that the war was at an end'.[8]

Although a strong party existed in the Scottish Parliament which wished to maintain monarchical government there and was willing to support Charles's 'just title to the Crown in England', their commissioners in that country had no intention of breaking with their allies at Westminster, as the Marquis of Argyll, the most powerful man in Scotland, was careful to make clear to the two Houses of Parliament when he visited London towards the end of June; he accepted without a quibble the terms that had been drawn up and subsequently brought to Newcastle by English commissioners, embodying the price that Charles was required to pay for resuming his seat on the throne of England, but as a 'regulated' or constitutional monarch. He was asked to deliver the control of the army and navy to Parliament for twenty years, to allow Parliament to nominate the chief officers of State and the judges, to accept the exemption of many leading Royalists from pardon for the part they had taken in the civil war, to agree to the imposition of severe penalties upon all English Roman Catholics who openly practised their religion, and to consent to the permanent abolition of episcopacy. While Charles was utterly determined to reject such conditions as a whole, he attempted to spin out the negotiations about them as long as he possibly could. He had first endeavoured to pacify his Scottish jailers by asking them to invite their leading theologian, Alexander Henderson, to come to Newcastle from London in order to instruct him in the nature of the Presbyterian faith – though, according to Clarendon's *History* Charles was 'too hard for him in argumentation' – and Henderson soon left for Edinburgh to die of grief there at his failure to convert the King. Charles next tried to persuade the English Parliamentarian commissioners of his desire:

> . . . that he might be removed to some of his own houses and that he might reside there till upon a personal treaty with his Parliament such an agreement might be established as the kingdom might enjoy peace under it, which he was sure it could never do by the concessions they proposed.

During the autumn Charles was vehemently pressed by the Queen and by some of his former ministers who were still at liberty including Sir John Culpeper, his Master of the Rolls, Digby, his Secretary of State, and Lord Jermyn, the Queen's major-domo, to accept a Presbyterian Church of England in return for his restoration to the throne. Another French ambassador, who was sent to England by Cardinal Mazarin, learned in London that nothing could be done to help the King unless he gave up his episcopal Church and granted all the lands belonging to the cathedrals to such uses as Parliament should advise. The Queen also ordered William Davenant, a witty poet reputedly the illegitimate son of William Shakespeare, to go to Newcastle to induce Charles to change his mind on the Church question, but he was sent packing. Charles did, however, put forward an offer to grant Presbyterian supremacy for three or even five years if after that a regulated episcopacy was restored, and he also volunteered to abandon control over the armed forces for ten years or even for the rest of his life. Henriette Marie was adamantly opposed to her husband giving way over the control of the armed forces, but considered that if his conscience permitted him to accept Presbyterianism for a limited time, he might just as well accept it in perpetuity provided the concession saved him his throne. Charles retorted: 'if the pulpits teach not obedience (which will never be if Presbyterianism be absolutely established) the King will have but small comfort

Queen Henriette Marie: a painting after Van Dyck, c. 1632–5. She left Charles in 1644 and did not return to England again until her eldest son succeeded to the throne

of the militia'. In fact, his marriage, which had once given him so much happiness, was breaking down. Henriette Marie threatened never to set foot in England again, said she would only pray for him, and warned him not to try to escape to France – that would be far too dangerous. In return he assured her that he was a prisoner who could not escape, but insisted that if the Prince of Wales, who was now with her in Paris, were to grant more in his name to the English Parliament than would satisfy his own conscience, 'I shall not live long after.'[9]

Charles's hope – one among many – that he could play off the Scottish government against the English Parliament soon evaporated. Even his final concessions failed to impress his Scottish captors, while the leaders of the Parliament at Westminster, who ever since his arrival at Newcastle had been anxious to get him into their power – though forbidding him to come to London under honourable conditions – arranged a settlement whereby in return for a payment of £400,000 to meet their expenses for taking part in the civil war the Covenanters agreed to withdraw all the troops and garrisons from England. By 11 February 1647 every Scottish soldier, therefore, crossed the river Tweed making for home. The Covenanters never contemplated taking King Charles away with them or allowing him to escape once they were convinced that he had no intention of consenting to the permanent establishment of a strict Presbyterian Church similar to their own beloved Kirk as supreme in England. Commissioners, headed by the aged and bad-tempered Earl of Pembroke, who had once been his Lord Chamberlain, arrived at Newcastle in mid-January and took charge of Charles. Thus, on 3 February he left the town where he had been so deeply miserable as the prisoner of the victorious Parliamentarians, nearly a year and a half after the decisive battle at Naseby.

11 King Charles the Prisoner

Recognizing after the surrender of Oxford and the defeat of the Marquis of Montrose in Scotland that he had no immediate prospect of regaining his authority by warfare Charles concentrated his hopes for his future on negotiating a peaceful settlement by dividing his enemies. Although modern academic historians have drawn subtle distinctions between 'religious' and 'political' Presbyterians and 'religious' and 'political' Independents confronting one another in the House of Commons all the contemporaries who wrote about them, including the French ambassadors in England, the King himself, the future Earl of Clarendon and Denzil Holles, the chief advocate of a constitutional settlement, were perfectly satisfied with describing them simply as the two rival political groups which the Royalists believed they could play off against each other. Similarly, the Scottish leaders were divided between the followers of the saturnine Marquis of Argyll, a rigorous supporter of the English Parliamentarians, known as the Covenanters, and those who were loyal to the Duke of Hamilton and his brother, the Earl of Lanark, known as Royalists or Engagers: they had not wanted the Scottish army stationed in Newcastle upon Tyne to hand over the person of the King to the English commissioners, who came to fetch him into their custody.

As arranged before the Scots left Newcastle, these commissioners – three peers and six members of the House of Commons – carried Charles south, well out of the reach of Scotland, to his stately mansion at Holdenby in Nottinghamshire, commonly called Holmby House, a journey of 180 miles taking thirteen days. On the way there crowds gathered to watch the King passing, mostly 'with acclamations of joy and with prayers for his preservation'.[1] Once he arrived at Holmby he was disappointed that he was not allowed to have his own chaplains or grooms of the bedchamber and was obliged to say grace at meals himself and 'sequester himself' to his private devotions on Sundays. But he had ample time to reflect quietly about the future. According to a report by the French ambassador in London written just before Charles came to Holmby:

Archibald Campbell, 8th Earl and 1st Marquis of Argyll (1598–1661): a painting by David Scougall

The King was resolved to do nothing in order to give peace to the kingdom and that he was certain that by taking patience for six months everything will be upset so that his affairs would arrange themselves without his having anything to do with them.[2]

While Charles enjoyed placidly walking in the gardens at Holmby, playing chess or visiting neighbouring estates for a game of bowls, he learned that at Westminster Parliament was indeed divided among its members about a constitutional settlement and was at cross-purposes with its army, while in Scotland Parliament was equally divided between the supporters of the Marquis of Argyll and the Duke of Hamilton, the latter being ready to compromise on religious matters if that was the only way of helping their King. The Presbyterian majority in the House of Commons proposed that the bulk of the New Model Army should be sent to Ireland to suppress the Roman Catholic Confederate forces there and that only a relatively small garrison should be retained in England under the command of General Fairfax, while no other officer should hold a rank higher than that of colonel. This was obviously a deliberate insult to Oliver Cromwell, the real victor at Naseby. Cromwell told Fairfax that there were 'in all places men who have so much malice against the army as besots them', and he actually entered into negotiations with the Elector Palatine, Prince Rupert's eldest brother, 'to transfer himself with as many of the victors of Naseby as he could carry with him to the battlefields of Germany'.[3] Nothing came of this, however, and in the middle of May, despite the fact that members of the House of Commons had passed without a division (in the absence of many Independents) what came to be known as a 'Declaration of Dislike'[4] of the army, condemning the soldiers for petitioning Fairfax about their grievances and describing them as 'enemies of the State and disturbers of the public peace' Oliver agreed to go with his son-in-law, Ireton, and two other members of parliament to the army headquarters so as to quieten the 'distempers' of the officers and soldiers there. What the petition to Fairfax had asked for was an indemnity for actions considered to be illegal committed by soldiers during the war, security for their arrears of pay, provision for men badly injured in the fighting, and pensions for widows and orphans of men who had been killed.

So indignant was the bulk of the New Model Army at its treatment by the majority in the House of Commons that Cromwell and his fellow commissioners were unable to pacify it. 'Is it not better to die like men than to be enslaved and hanged like dogs?' asked the private soldiers. Though the petitioners had not put forward any political or religious demands, some troopers in the cavalry regiments who first elected agents or 'Agitators', as they came to be called, to express the views of the rank-and-file, were actually reported to have claimed that they had 'fought all this time to bring the King to London and to London they will bring the King'.[5]

Charles soon became aware of the growing conflict between the majority in the Commons and the discontented majority in the army. For that reason he occupied his leisure in drawing up an answer to the Newcastle propositions, which had again been submitted to him by the commissioners at Holmby during April. He accepted the imposition of a Presbyterian State Church for three years pending an agreed religious settlement and consented to the control of the armed forces by Parliament for ten years, but asked to be allowed to come to Westminster in order to give his assent to the Bills needed to legalize such a deal.

The volatile state of the New Model Army and its reluctance to serve in Ireland had deeply perturbed the Parliamentarians, headed by Denzil Holles in the House of Commons; they therefore treated Charles's latest proposals seriously and favourably. At the same time some influential officers including Cromwell began to consider whether they also might be able to come to terms with the King. Consequently Parliament and the army sought direct contact with him. The army leaders feared that Charles, who was under the guard of a Presbyterian Major-General and a Presbyterian Colonel at Holmby, might be moved away from there and it was speculated that the intention was to take him to Scotland to lead an army to confront the New Model. Whether that was true or not, both Houses of Parliament resolved to give the soldiers in the New

Model a choice between volunteering for Ireland or being disbanded instantly. This choice was to be presented to each regiment, beginning on 1 June.

As soon as the decision was known General Fairfax received a petition from the Agitators asking him to call a general rendezvous of his army to agree on a demand that all their grievances should be met before the disbandment took place. Fairfax accepted the request and soldiers belonging to thirteen regiments gathered on Kentford Heath near Newmarket including officers, non-commissioned officers and Agitators representing the privates; here on 4 and 5 June a Solemn Engagement was assented to, which set up what became known as a General Council of the Army to achieve the redress of their grievances and hinted at political aims.

At the same time these Agitators had undertaken more positive action. A party of 500 cavalrymen under the command of Cornet George Joyce had ridden to Holmby, fraternized with the small garrison there, and ordered the King to leave Northamptonshire and place himself in the hands of the Army. Charles, though surprised, acquiesced and asked if he might be taken to his hunting lodge at Newmarket and that the Parliamentarian commissioners who had been with him at Holmby should accompany him. The King, wrote Sir Thomas Herbert (whom Parliament had appointed to be one of his grooms of the bedchamber at Holmby) 'was the merriest of the company having [it seems] a confidence in the Army, especially some of the greatest there . . '..[6]

On his way to Newmarket Charles met Fairfax and Cromwell near Cambridge, where the army headquarters was now stationed. Both of them denied that they had had anything to do with Joyce's exploit, though Charles did not believe them. He arrived at Newmarket on 8 June and remained there for a

Medals of Cromwell and Fairfax produced in Holland

fortnight. During that time the hostility between the leaders of the Commons and the New Model Army sharpened to such an extent that open warfare between them was threatened. Denzil Holles aimed to create a rival army raised in London where the City authorities favoured a peaceful settlement with the King by calling upon the trained bands, which numbered 18,000 men, to be directed by a militia committee from which the Independents were excluded, enlisting disbanded soldiers known as 'Reformadoes' and calling upon the help of 'mechanic citizens'.[7]

Holles and other Presbyterian leaders in the Commons demanded that the King should be sent back to Holmby and, when this was refused, that he should be brought to Richmond in Surrey so as to be out of reach of the New Model Army and within easy reach of Westminster. Charles expressed his willingness to go there, but Fairfax and Cromwell did not intend to allow the King to escape from their guard. They were firm in their resistance to Holles and his colleagues, who had made little progress with their attempt to 'exhort the citizens [of London] to defend themselves against the mad men in the Army'.[8] A *Declaration of the Army* was drawn up on 14 June in which clearly political ends were advocated. It required the two Houses of Parliament to be purged of members who misconducted themselves, asked that a reformed Parliament should be called in the near future, and required that the King's rights should be settled once and for all. This was in effect an ultimatum. Although on 23 June the Commons rejected the terms of the *Declaration* the Presbyterian leaders realized that their scheme for recruiting a makeshift army of their own had collapsed since the idea of a 'White Guard' of the revolution had so frightened the City of London that it retreated into neutrality, while the mere advance of the New Model Army to Uxbridge, north-west of London, was sufficient to compel Holles and his colleagues to withdraw from the House of Commons. Instead of moving his troops on to Westminster Fairfax withdrew them to Reading where the General Council of the Army met for the first time. Here Lieutenant-General Cromwell, Major-General John Lambert, Commissary-General Ireton and a number of civilian Independents drew up a document known as the *Heads of the Proposals* in the hope that it would prove acceptable both to the King and to the House of Commons, would be 'firm and durable' and 'avoid the great objection,' as Cromwell urged, 'that will lie against us that we have got things out of Parliament by force'.[9]

The *Heads of the Proposals* provided for a House of Commons to be elected every two years by reformed constituencies, for the control of the armed forces to be in the hands of Parliament for ten years, for the great officers of State to be appointed by Parliament also for ten years, and for considerable authority to be conferred on a Council of State which would replace the old Privy Council.

Episcopacy was to be retained but the coercive power of the bishops was to be taken away and toleration granted to all Christians except 'Papists and Popish recusants' who 'disturbed the State'. Certain other reforms relating to taxation and the law were also advocated in general terms. During the summer of 1647 the King was shuffled about between various noblemen's houses in accordance with the movement of the army. It was when he was at Woburn, the Earl of Bedford's famous mansion, on 20 July that Cromwell and Ireton first discussed the *Heads of the Proposals* with him and even consented to moderate them in response to some of Charles's objections. But Charles took an immediate dislike to them and told Sir John Berkeley 'they would never impose so hard terms on him'. He instructed Berkeley and Ashburnham, who were both with him again, to promise Cromwell and any of his friends 'advantages to themselves' if they procured his 're-establishment'. Berkeley, however, thought that 'never was a Crown (that had been so near lost) so cheaply recovered as his Majesty's would be, if they agreed upon such terms'. Ashburnham, on the other hand, agreed with Charles and believed he could buy the services of Cromwell and Ireton, blaming the part of the *Proposals* which the King disliked on the activities of the Agitators who were clearly 'senseless fellows'. Charles was also convinced that he could play off the army against the Presbyterian party in the House of Commons and the City of London; he told Cromwell and Ireton: 'You cannot do without me; you will fall to ruin if I do not sustain you'.[10]

Two days before the *Heads of the Proposals* were presented to the King in their final form by a deputation from the army the Presbyterian majority in the House of Commons began a last effort to defy Fairfax and the New Model Army. Most of the eleven members proscribed by the army had returned to their seats and on 2 August both Houses of Parliament, under pressure from City mobs, voted in favour of bringing the King to London to engage in peace negotiations. It seemed momentarily as if a new war would break out between the forces in the City under the command of Colonel Edward Massey, an experienced officer with Presbyterian leanings and dubious morals, and the New Model Army. Undoubtedly that was why Charles rejected the *Heads of the Proposals* as they stood since he felt confident of obtaining better terms from one side or the other. But the New Model Army had the leading role in the drama. Fifty-eight members of the House of Commons and eight from the House of Lords, terrified by the tumults in the City, sought the protection of General Fairfax and his army. The City soon succumbed and abandoned the intention of entering on a new war. Fairfax brought the fugitive members of the two Houses to Westminster and posted forces both to guard the Houses of Parliament and the Tower of London. For the second time an attempt to defy the New Model Army with a 'White Guard' of counter-revolutionaries had failed. Fairfax and his

Council of War then issued a declaration saying: 'We shall be ready to assure unto the King his just rights and authority'.[11]

Charles was now at Stoke Park in Buckinghamshire. He was there asked by Cromwell and Ireton 'since his Majesty would not yield to the Proposals yet he should at least send a kind letter to the Army before it was commonly known that London would submit'.[12] They were anxious for Charles to demonstrate that he had not supported the tumultuous pressures in the City to secure his being brought back there to negotiate a settlement. Charles hesitated about doing so and delayed finally repudiating any responsibility for the disorders in the capital, motivated on his behalf, until after the City had surrendered to Fairfax. The French ambassador in London, an impartial observer, wrote on 5 August, the day after the surrender, that the King

> . . . has lost during the last ten days the opportunity of re-establishing himself. He could have done so by means of the City before it joined itself to Parliament, and also done so very advantageously through the Army, had he come to terms with it eight days ago, as it eagerly wished and he was advised to do. His natural irresolution, together with the hope he and his council have always been too much led by, that matters would have become disordered so that one would be obliged to grant him good conditions, has caused him to lose up till now many advantages that have been offered to him.[13]

Although Charles had been assured that if he would agree to the army's *Proposals* Parliament would be obliged to accept them he continued to reject them himself. He had asked permission to move from Stoke Park to one of his own houses and had been allowed to go to Oatlands, a large and comfortable house belonging to the Queen on the banks of the River Thames. Although Cromwell and Ireton had acquiesced in his doing so they warned Ashburnham 'that they had met with sufficient proof that the King had not only abetted and fomented the difficulties between them and their enemies', but had entered into negotiations with the Scots. In fact, the Earl of Lauderdale, after he had seen the King at Woburn, had been expelled by the soldiers.

Charles was again 'very merry' while housed at Oatlands, but on 24 August he was transferred to Hampton Court palace shortly after Fairfax brought his army headquarters to Putney. Within a fortnight of Charles settling in at Hampton Court the House of Commons, though purged of its Presbyterian leaders once again, sent the King the propositions of Newcastle as amended in the House of Lords. Cromwell and Ireton and evidently some of the leading Independents naturally hoped that these stiffer terms for a settlement, terms that the King had already rejected three times, would make him more amenable to the army's *Proposals*, which he had also rejected. According to Ashburnham, who was with the King at Hampton Court, 'Cromwell and Ireton desired that the King should not be discouraged for they would never give over the thoughts of serving him,

Hampton Court palace: a painting by an unknown artist, c. 1640. King Charles was taken there as a prisoner of the Parliamentarian army in 1647

although there were but six men of the whole Army to stand by them.' The difficulty from their point of view was that not only did Charles persist in refusing to consent to the army's scheme for a settlement and continue to desire 'a personal treaty', but there was growing opposition, chiefly from the Agitators in the General Council of the Army, to the *Heads of the Proposals* as being too favourable to the King; Oliver Cromwell was actually accused of being 'a courtier'.

How far the Levellers, a group of radicals centred mainly in London and headed by John Lilburne, a former lieutenant-colonel, and by John Wildman, who was frequently described as a major (nobody quite knows why), were responsible for influencing the strong opposition from many officers and soldiers to the *Heads of the Proposals* is uncertain, but undoubtedly a document entitled an *Agreement of the People*, which was largely drawn up by Wildman that autumn, envisaged the establishment of a democratic and egalitarian society implicitly without a monarchy or House of Lords. Trooper Edward Sexby, who opened a debate on this *Agreement*, declared that the army's misery was caused by labouring to please a King who would never be satisfied and upholding a Parliament that consisted of rotten members. Cromwell and Ireton firmly repudiated the idea that they had been plotting to satisfy the King.

In fact, during September when Charles was at Hampton Court and the army headquarters were at Putney Cromwell had tried hard to persuade the King to accept the *Heads of the Proposals*, had supported his reiterated request to come to London to negotiate about his future, and had resisted a motion put forward in the House of Commons that no further addresses should be made to the King. Not only had he and Ireton sent frequent messages to Charles from Putney, but they and their wives had visited him at Hampton Court and admired the devotion he showed to his younger children who were allowed to see him there. Later, however, during the debates in the General Council of the Army during October Cromwell complained to Ashburnham 'that the King could not be trusted and that he had no affection to or confidence in the Army'. In his memoirs Ashburnham recalled that Cromwell and Ireton were

> . . . at so great a distance to what they had appeared to be in relation to His Majesty's good, as I was clearly confirmed that there was no more to be hoped for from them, unless pure necessity by an absolute breach with Parliament enforced them.[14]

So Charles resolved that it was in his best interests to escape from the power of the army, just as he had previously got away from his Scottish Covenanter captors at Newcastle and then allowed himself to be kidnapped, without complaining, from his Parliamentarian custodians at Holmby. He had already been assured by the Scottish commissioners headed by the Earl of Lauderdale, who saw him again at Hampton Court on 22 October, that he could rely on support from Scotland to recover his throne provided that he satisfied the Parliament there on the subject of religion. Next day he was urged to escape with the commissioners to Scotland or at any rate to accompany them as far as Berwick-upon-Tweed, but he said grandly that he had given his word not to escape.

During the first week of November Charles must have learnt that in the discussions in the General Council of the Army at Putney the New Model representatives had been extremely mixed in their feelings towards him: as where foot soldiers in two regiments had declared they were loyal to him, others had shown a distinct animus against him.[15] For instance Colonel Thomas Harrison, later to become an enthusiastic republican, asserted at Putney that Charles was 'a man of blood'.

The King was warned both by an anonymous letter that has been attributed to a brother of 'Freeborn John Lilburne', the celebrated leader of the Levellers, and by a letter from Cromwell that 'there were rumours of some intended attempt on his Majesty's person'. This second letter was received on 11 November by Colonel Edward Whalley, who was in charge at Hampton Court and was Cromwell's first cousin. Whalley showed it to the King. But before that Charles had already made up his mind to escape. Although both he and John Ashburnham (who, together with Sir John Berkeley, was expelled from the palace by Whalley on 1 November) had given their parole not to escape, and since, as Whalley himself admitted, Hampton Court's 1,500 rooms meant that he 'could no more keep the King there if he had a mind to go than a bird in a pound', Charles had no difficulty in arranging on 3 November with Berkeley,

Ashburnham, and Sir William Legge, the former Governor of Oxford, who had been allowed to remain with him after the other two had been expelled, to make preparations for his escape. This was achieved easily enough on the evening of 11 November. Whether, as Berkeley stated in his memoirs, the King 'was really afraid of his life by the tumultuous part of the Army' or, as Charles wrote in a message he left for Whalley, this was not the reason for his flight is a matter of small importance, but it was typical of Charles that after he had been persuaded to escape, he was undecided where he was going.[16]

One or two historians have claimed that Oliver Cromwell deliberately instigated Charles's flight from Hampton Court and had actually earlier visited the Isle of Wight, where the King was finally to arrive from the mainland, to take precautions against such an eventuality. This story – like the story that Cromwell had instigated Cornet Joyce's seizure of the King at Holmby – implies that he was an intriguer, 'the greatest dissembler living', as Clarendon called him, whose ultimate intention was to replace Charles as the ruler of England, Scotland and Ireland. That is so contrary to Oliver Cromwell's generally accepted reputation as an honourable Christian statesman that it is hard to credit and anyhow the evidence is suspect. It was Charles not Cromwell who struggled by every devious means left at his disposal after his defeat at Naseby to plot in any way he could think of for his restoration to power.

Indeed, as John Ashburnham argued after Charles's martyrdom (admittedly in making his own defence):

> It was not the King's remove from Hampton Court into the Isle of Wight . . . that brought the evil fate upon him . . . for after being there he had by the entrance of the Duke of Hamilton's army) according to the Agreement in the Isle of Wight [and] by the Insurrections in Kent, Essex, Wales and Pomfrett [Pontefract Castle] far greater hopes of being restored than ever he had whilst in person in Arms.[17]

This was the course taken by the second civil war which began in 1648.

12 The Second Civil War

Charles's behaviour in planning his flight from Hampton Court palace to the Isle of Wight throws a flood of light on to his character. It was both devious and confused. As has been noted, he did not welcome the suggestion put forward by the Scottish commissioners, who visited him at Hampton Court during the first week of October 1647 and had, in fact, fifty cavalrymen with them, that he should accompany them to Berwick or Edinburgh, because he insisted he must honour his promise not to escape. Yet fewer than five weeks later he ordered John Ashburnham to invent some excuse to repudiate his parole. Secondly, as has been noted, he was undecided where to go. As always, he would have liked to make his way to Westminster so as to plead his cause personally before the Houses of Parliament. Ashburnham actually offered to carry him up to London where he would arrange for him to meet the Scottish commissioners in the Lord Mayor's Mansion House and try to persuade them and the Presbyterian party in the City to come to terms with him about his restoration to authority. If that failed, he could still sail overseas. When Sir John Berkeley was consulted about this scheme, he thought it extremely dangerous and it was given up.[1]

To begin with, Charles had contemplated the idea of taking himself to the island of Jersey, but later thought it wiser not to move so far away from the heart of his kingdom; instead he acquiesced in the next proposal by Ashburnham that he should make for the Isle of Wight, where the Parliamentarian military Governor was Colonel Robert Hammond, who was a nephew of Henry Hammond, one of the King's former chaplains and was believed (wrongly) to be sympathetic to Charles. Had Ashburnham managed to procure a suitable ship Charles might still have elected to go to Jersey or to France; Berkeley was indeed asked to find one, but was not able to do so in time. So instead Charles sent Ashburnham and Berkeley from Titchfield House on Southampton water, which they reached on 12 November, to interview Hammond in the Isle of Wight. But against his orders they brought the governor back with them. Charles was not at all pleased. 'With a very severe and reserved countenance', he said it was too late to 'boggle' and refused Ashburnham's offer to assassinate Hammond and reluctantly agreed to accompany the Colonel from Titchfield to Carisbrooke Castle near Newport in the centre of the Isle of Wight. Basically what Charles wanted was to find himself a haven out of easy reach of both the English Parliament and the English army where he could enjoy more freedom to negotiate for his restoration. Safe from direct pressure he thought he might be able to play off the representatives of Parliament, the leaders of the army and the Scottish commissioners against one another and exact the best terms possible.

Five days after Charles settled in Carisbrooke Castle under the care of Colonel Hammond he sent a conciliatory message to the Houses of Parliament stating that he was ready to agree to the retention of a Presbyterian Church of England for three years so long as he himself and those who could not conscientiously accept it were allowed their own religious practices. He also said he would consent to the control of the army and navy being given to Parliament for the remainder of his own lifetime, to the right of Parliament to nominate Ministers of State and Privy Councillors for the whole of his reign, and to the suppression of all the declarations that he had published against the Parliamentarians. Finally he sought for an Act of Oblivion for all his subjects; and he

King Charles I in Carisbrooke Castle on the Isle of Wight, where he was a prisoner during 1648, as pictured in a Royalist broadsheet of the time

recommended the plan earlier put forward by the New Model Army for the holding of regular parliaments and for electoral reform. As usual, he asked for permission to come to London himself so that these concessions could be worked out, his reasonable requests examined, and a firm peace concluded.

This was the most extensive surrender of his prerogatives adumbrated by King Charles since his defeat at the battle of Naseby. Though members of parliament and army officers were naturally suspicious about his behaviour since his flight from Hampton Court people at large in England were pleased by this royal message and the Scottish commissioners still in London strongly approved of his request for a personal treaty there. As Gardiner wrote, 'those who had most to gain by the restoration of order and the disbandment of the army welcomed Charles's message as in every way satisfactory'.[2] It certainly encouraged the defeated Cavaliers. The French ambassador in London reported home that the King seemed to have granted everything that had been asked of him and had given hope that any questions not dealt with in his message could easily be settled by a personal treaty.[3] Was he sincere?

The Parliament in London took its time in replying to Charles's latest offer. Then four Bills were drawn up. The first gave the control of the armed forces to Parliament for twenty years; the second revoked all royal declarations against Parliament, thus identifying the King expressly as the author of the civil war; the third annulled all titles of peerage bestowed by the King since May 1642 and declared that no further peerages could be created without the consent of the two Houses; and the fourth gave the present Parliament the right to adjourn itself to any place it thought fit. If Charles agreed to the enactment of these Bills he would then be permitted to come to London to settle any outstanding questions ranging from the abolition of the bishops to the exemption of specific 'delinquents' – that is to say men like Prince Rupert who had fought in the Royalist armies – from an Act of Oblivion. It was, in fact, the list of propositions that would need to be discussed after Charles assented to the four Bills – embodying demands that had been asked from him at Newcastle and elsewhere – which were certain to prove unacceptable to him.

On 24 December 1647 a joint committee from the two Houses of Parliament, headed by the 2nd Earl of Denbigh, brought the text of the four Bills to Carisbrooke. Next day Scottish commissioners including the Earls of Lauderdale, Loudoun and Lanark, who had previously seen the King several times at Hampton Court, also arrived at Carisbrooke. They had deliberately set off in the wake of the English commissioners pretending they were merely coming to the Isle of Wight to deliver a condemnation of the proceedings of the English Parliament and army as being contrary to the terms of the Solemn League and Covenant between the two kingdoms. They were not unduly worried about the liberties of Englishmen, but were planning secretly and independently to arrange a separate agreement with the King of Scotland. Charles was delighted. On 26 December he rapidly entered into an Engagement with the Scots and two days later he refused to sign the four Bills.

By the Engagement the King undertook to confirm in a free parliament the Solemn League and Covenant of 1643 which provided for 'the nearest conjunction and uniformity between England and Scotland' along Presbyterian lines, but did not oblige either Charles or his subjects to take it; a Presbyterian Church was to be confirmed in England for three years and all nonconformist opinions and practices were to be suppressed. In return the Kingdom of Scotland engaged 'in a peaceful manner to endeavour that His Majesty may come to London to make a peaceful treaty with the Houses of Parliament and the Commissioners of Scotland, all armies being disbanded'. Otherwise an army would be sent from Scotland to England to defend the King's personal authority and secure a lasting peace. Charles also promised to aim at a complete union between his two kingdoms and to ensure equal treatment for Scotsmen with Englishmen in his service during the future.[4]

Thus, by his stubborness at Newcastle, Holmby and Hampton Court, Charles had succeeded in defying the extreme demands of the English Parliament and army and by granting minimum concessions himself extracted a promise from the Scottish Engagers that they would uphold his traditional prerogatives of command over the English armed forces, of the right to choose his own ministers and councillors, to confer honours, and to exercise a veto over the enactments of Parliament. If a Scottish army proved able to fulfil the terms of the Engagement Charles would have won almost as great a triumph as if he had been victorious at the battle of Naseby. According to Ashburnham, after concluding the Engagement Charles hoped 'to get into France, from whence he might wait advantages by the promised army from Scotland'.[5] So while Colonel Hammond was away from Carisbrooke Castle, seeing off the party from the two Houses of Parliament at Newport which had brought the four rejected Bills, the King planned to embark on a French ship that had by now been hired for him and awaited him at Southampton. It was there on 29 December. But the wind changed direction so that a vessel that would have carried him over to catch it at Southampton was unable to sail.

Up to this time King Charles had been at liberty to ride about the whole of the island wherever he liked, to enjoy the company of the three courtiers who had come with him from Hampton Court as well as servants of his from Oxford, only his chaplains being denied him; but now, following his refusal of the four Bills, he was confined to the castle grounds where he could only exercise himself by walking or playing bowls. The actual text of the Engagement was enclosed in lead and hidden elsewhere on the island, but naturally the Parliamentarians were suspicious about Charles's meetings with the Scottish Commissioners and therefore the English army took every precaution to prevent him from escaping again. For their part the Scottish Commissioners calmly returned to London where they entered into secret discussions with Royalist sympathizers. But since, as Clarendon wrote, even before they left London they 'gave such constant advertisements of the impatience of their countrymen to be in arms for the King'[6] and as during Christmas there were demonstrations by rioters in favour of the King in different parts of the country, largely because they were tiring of Puritan austerities, on 3 January 1648 the House of Commons voted by 141 to 91 that no further addresses should be made to him.

Oliver Cromwell, now temporarily transmuted from soldier into politician, who took part in the debate, expressed his distrust of Charles as 'an obstinate man whose heart God had hardened', but did not condemn monarchy as such. On that same day he wrote to Colonel Hammond: 'the House of Commons is very sensible of the King's dealings . . . You should do well if you have anything that may discover juggling, to search it out and let us know'.[7] The General Council of the Army also declared its support for ending negotiations with the King and finally a few members of the House of Lords concurred. Suspicion of the Scots Commissioners was reflected in a decision taken at the same time to dissolve the Committee of Both Kingdoms which had supervised the waging of the first civil war from London since 1643. The Scots Commissioners left London on 24 January; in mid-February they persuaded the Committee of Estates at Edinburgh to vote in favour of the Engagement, although they were opposed by the Marquis of Argyll and other noblemen. At the beginning of March the Scottish Parliament approved of the Engagement by a majority of thirty-five votes. Thus the way was opened for a second civil war.

But the activities of a revivified Royalist party and of the Scottish Engagers which launched the war were never effectively coordinated. Possibly if Charles had managed to get away from his close imprisonment on the Isle of Wight that might have helped. But three attempts to escape from Carisbrooke Castle, the first immediately after his signature of the Engagement, the second on 20 March 1648 when his body got stuck in his chamber window when attempting to drop on to the ground below, and the last on 28 May when two sentries who had been suborned betrayed him, all failed.

The initial military action in the new war took place as early as 23 March, when Colonel John Poyer, the Governor of Pembroke Castle in Wales, seized the neighbouring castle of Tenby and aided by discontented Parliamentarian soldiers declared for the King. Oliver Cromwell, soldier again, was promptly dispatched by General Fairfax to South Wales, where Pembroke Castle

A

DECLARATION

OF THE

COMMONS

OF

ENGLAND

In PARLIAMENT affembled ;

EXPRESSING

Their Reafons and Grounds of paffing
the late Refolutions touching

No farther Addrefs or Application to be made

TO THE

KING.

Die Veneris, 11. Februarii, 1647.

ORdered by the *Commons affembled in Parliament,* That this *Declaration* be *forthwith*
printed and publifhed :

H. Elfynge, Cler. Parl. D. Com.

London, Printed for *Edw. Husband,* Printer to the
Honourable Houfe of Commons, *Feb.* 15. 1647.

*On the eve of the second civil war the House of Commons voted that no further addresses should be
made to the King. This declaration was published on 11 February 1648 (the year was then reckoned
to begin in March)*

A medal from 1645 depicting Sir Thomas Fairfax, who succeeded his father as Lord Fairfax of Cameron, a Scottish title

surrendered to him on 11 July; Poyer, who, Cromwell stated, had 'sinned against so much light and against so many evidences of God's presence', was later shot dead as a mutineer. Meanwhile, by the beginning of June Fairfax had suppressed a Royalist rising in Kent and then in mid-June began besieging Colchester, where 4,000 Royalists who had escaped from Kent held out until the end of August, when they were starved into surrender and their leaders executed.

Thus the Royalist revolts in England and Wales had been practically crushed before the Scottish Engagers crossed into England on 8 July. The reason why they had delayed until then was that the decision to raise an army to fight for King Charles had been condemned not only by the Marquis of Argyll and other members of the Presbyterian nobility but also by the Kirk, which urged that whereas the English Parliament had been blamed for failing to fulfil the terms of the Solemn League and Covenant, the King had not been asked to impose the Covenant on the English people. What was even more disconcerting to the Duke of Hamilton at the head of the Engagers was that several of the best qualified Scottish officers, including the Earl of Leven, General David Leslie and

Major-General John Holborne, all of whom had fought with Fairfax and Cromwell in the first civil war, refused to join his army. Another of Hamilton's disappointments was that his request that the Prince of Wales, who had been with his mother in France, should come to Scotland to take nominal command of the invading army was not accepted. Prince Charles – who was then eighteen years old – had for various reasons hesitated to come and, in fact, he had been welcomed as Admiral of part of the Parliamentarian navy which had revolted during the summer and sailed to Holland where he joined it. Had these mutinous sailors been willing to take their warships to Scotland they might materially have assisted Hamilton. But they insisted on entering the Thames to capture rich prizes. So the Prince of Wales was compelled to stay with them.

The chief aid that Hamilton acquired from the revived Royalist movement was the occupation of Berwick-upon-Tweed and Carlisle by English soldiers under the omnipresent Marmaduke Langdale, whom Cromwell had defeated at the battle of Naseby, and Sir Philip Musgrave, who had been appointed Governor of Carlisle by Charles I during the first civil war. Though these strategic towns had been seized by the Royalists in April it was not until July that the Duke of Hamilton had overcome his immense difficulties in recruiting an army of some 17,000 men to lead into England. As it was, by 12 August Cromwell had collected 'a fine smart army fit for action' of 9,000 men after he joined Major-General Lambert, who had been in charge of the Parliamentarian forces in the north of England since the beginning of the year. It is true that Hamilton had in addition to the 17,000 men he had raised in Scotland the Royalists under Langdale and a contingent of 3,000 Scots who came over from northern Ireland giving him a total force of at least 27,000 soldiers with whom to confront Cromwell and Lambert. However, as his Quartermaster-General, Sir James Turner wrote:

> The weakness, rawness and undisciplinedness of our soldiers, our want of artillery and horse to carry the little ammunition we had, the constant rainy, stormy and tempestuous weather which attended us, which made all the highways impassable for man and beast, our want of intelligence, our leaving our Irish auxiliaries so far behind us, and our unfortunate resolution to waive Yorkshire and march by Lancashire all . . . made us prey to Cromwell's veteran army.[8]

The Duke of Hamilton had decided to advance through Lancashire rather than Yorkshire in the hope of picking up more Royalist soldiers there. Langdale's men acted as an advance guard which later more by accident than design protected the left flank of the Scottish army. Because of the scarcity of supplies the invading forces were strung out along the route from what was then Westmorland through Lancashire so that Cromwell was able to cross the

The Scottish Royalist commander, James, 1st Duke of Hamilton: a portrait after Van Dyck dated 1640. He was defeated by Cromwell after the battle of Preston, and executed in March 1649

Pennines from Knaresborough in north Yorkshire, where he had met Lambert, and surprise Langdale's men almost unsupported on Preston Moor. The ground there was clogged with hedges and ditches, enabling Langdale to put up a gallant fight against Cromwell's cavalry, holding it up for four hours or more before his contingent was almost wiped out. Hamilton did what he could to help, but was persuaded to allow the bulk of his army to continue on its way across the river Ribble and make for Wigan and Warrington, where in appalling weather his infantry were defeated in detail. Hamilton and his cavalry such as it was got away as far as Staffordshire, where on 25 August the Duke surrendered; he was executed on 9 March 1649.

The day before the battle of Preston the Prince of Wales had at last agreed to terms for joining the Scottish army, though far too late, while the rebel part of the Parliamentarian fleet, consisting of about a dozen ships, tried to give aid to the Royalists besieged in Colchester, but accomplished nothing. They returned to Holland, where they came under the command of Prince Rupert who sent a frigate to the Isle of Wight when King Charles was making his last attempt to escape from captivity.

It is remarkable that while the Scottish Engagers were invading England – an invasion which must have been known to have been inspired and approved by Charles – a majority in the Houses of Parliament at Westminster, including a number of members called 'Royal Independents' or 'the middle group' by modern academic historians, decided to reopen peace negotiations with him. This was chiefly because the Presbyterian members in the Commons and the City of London authorities were deeply distrustful of the New Model Army, which had refused to obey the orders for demobilization it had been given earlier and had twice entered and overawed London and Westminster to impose its demands. As Clarendon put it: 'Many in the Parliament, as well as in the city, who were controlled and dispirited by the presence of the army, when they were at a distance appeared resolute and brisk in any contradiction and opposition in their counsels.'[9] While Cromwell marched north and Fairfax was in Kent, therefore, the Common Council of the City of London petitioned Parliament to enter again into negotiations with the King, and the Commons revoked the order banning the Presbyterian leaders impeached by the army from attending its sessions, and immediately after the battle of Preston repealed the Vote of No Addresses which had been passed six months earlier.

Even before the repeal of the Vote of No Addresses one member of the House of Lords and two members of the Commons arrived at Carisbrooke Castle to ask the King if he would be willing to resume the discussion of a personal treaty once again on the basis of the propositions offered to him at Newcastle and Hampton Court. Charles agreed to take part in a conference at Newport with such members of the Parliament at Westminster as should be nominated to come there. He undertook not to leave the island while the treaty was in progress or twenty days afterwards while Parliament allotted forty days for the duration of the peace conference.

In theory Charles might have been expected to be delighted at this turn of events. For he had been permitted to leave Carisbrooke Castle and stay with a friendly Royalist, Sir William Hopkins, who was master of the grammar school in Newport. Gentlemen of his Bedchamber, Grooms of his Bedchamber, equerries and chaplains joined him there, even his barber (he had not enjoyed a hair cut for several weeks) and clerks of the kitchen were appointed for his service. It is true that he was obliged to conduct his side of the negotiations by himself without any member of his staff being present, but he was in good health and cheerful. At the outset of the discussions he stipulated that nothing that was agreed should have any validity until a complete understanding had been reached on every point. Parliament was represented by fifteen commissioners; on the one hand, they included the Presbyterian Sir Denzil Holles, who had led the opposition to the army in the House of Commons, and on the other by Sir Henry Vane, the friend of Oliver Cromwell, an Independent, who, it has been suggested, would assume it was his duty to sabotage any agreement unacceptable to his friends in the Army. He was certainly unlikely to put much trust in the King. Although Charles, as usual, offered a number of concessions, his proposals on the organization of religion, which involved the suspension of episcopacy and the establishment of Presbyterianism for three years, but allowed those whose consciences could not submit to it to secure toleration and included a compromise about the sale of bishops' lands, were rejected by the House of Commons. Charles objected to the exemption of several of his chief supporters called 'delinquents' from a mooted Act of Oblivion, but volunteered to impose minor penalties upon them. Again his offers were rejected by the House of Commons.

It is questionable if Charles ever had any real hope of a successful outcome from the conference at Newport even though he had always sought direct dealings with the Houses of Parliament about the future constitution of his kingdom. On 7 October, after nineteen days out of the forty days had expired, he told his host, Sir William Hopkins: 'Notwithstanding my too great concessions already made' – these included the withdrawal of his declarations against Parliament, his plans for religion, and his acceptance of penalties on delinquents – 'I know that unless I shall make yet others which will directly make me no King I shall be at best a perpetual prisoner . . . my only hope is that now they believe I dare deny them nothing and so be less careful of their guards.'[10]

As Parliament agreed in mid-November to extend the time allotted for the duration of the conference at Newport Hopkins, who was entrusted with the arrangements for the King's escape, gained a longer period in which to help his master, while John Ashburnham, who had been excluded from attendance at Newport but remained nearby in Hampshire, had also been commanded by the King 'to provide a barque at Hastings in readiness to carry him into France'.[11] Ashburnham recorded in his memoirs that he had procured a ship docked at Hastings and horses to carry Charles there. But Colonel Hammond was fully aware of what was afoot and his security precautions were impeccable. So during the time Charles was at liberty in Newport he was unable to escape from the island.

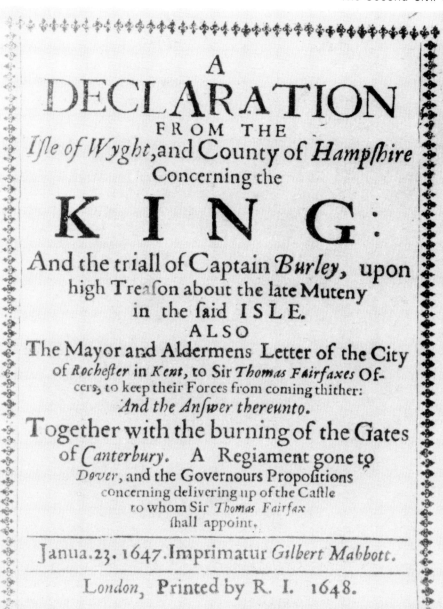

A

DECLARATION

F R O M   T H E
Iſle of Wyght, and County of *Hampſhire*
Concerning the

K I N G:

And the triall of Captain *Burley,* upon
high Treaſon about the late Muteny
in the ſaid I S L E.

A L S O

The Mayor and Aldermens Letter of the City
of *Rocheſter* in *Kent,* to Sir *Thomas Fairfaxes* Of-
cers, to keep their Forces from coming thither:
And the Anſwer thereunto.

Together with the burning of the Gates
of *Canterbury.*   A Regiament gone to
Dover, and the Governours Propoſitions
concerning delivering up of the Caſtle
to whom Sir *Thomas Fairfax*
ſhall appoint.

Janua. 23. 1647. Imprimatur *Gilbert Mabbott.*

London, Printed by R. I.   1648.

The front page of a newsletter which gives a short account of the trial of Captain John Burley, printed in 1648. Burley was one of the many who tried to organize an attempt to rescue the King from Carisbrooke Castle

Nevertheless, Charles had adumbrated a number of plausible concessions and also untruthfully promised to order the Marquis of Ormonde, who had returned to Ireland, to cease having any dealings with the Roman Catholic Confederation there, that is to say persuading the Irish to fight for him. His statements were carried back by the commissioners, who thought they were reasonably satisfactory, from Newport to Westminster. In bidding them farewell Charles said gloomily: 'God's will be done. I thank God I have made my peace with Him and shall without fear undergo what He shall suffer men to do unto me'.[12] At the same time he wrote to his son, the Prince of Wales, who had failed to persuade the fleet that had mutinied against Parliament to rescue his father or himself to join the Scottish Engagers, that he had laboured long for peace, but recognizing that since 'the English nation are a sober people, however at present infatuated' they would one day make him 'as great a prince as your father is a low one' and advised him if God gave him success to 'use it honourably and far from revenge'.[13]

Clearly Charles still harboured some vague hopes of military assistance from Ireland or France – though since the defeat of the Engagers by Cromwell help from Scotland seemed out of the question – but for once his habitual optimism deserted him, as can be seen from the tone of his letter to his son. Moreover, while the Parliamentarian commissioners had been treating with him in Newport a movement in the army manifested its distrust of the King. To use the term 'the army' is unsatisfactory. For General Fairfax, the Commander-in-Chief, was always anxious for a settlement between Parliament and the King and his wife was a crypto-Royalist. Oliver Cromwell, after settling affairs in Scotland following his defeat of the Engagers, was still in the north of England besieging Pontefract Castle and wrote: 'We wait upon the Lord who will teach us and lead us whether to doing or suffering'. The General Council of the Army, which had contained representatives of the common soldiers, had ceased to exist and it was the Council of Officers or the Council of the Army under the chairmanship of Fairfax that took the political decisions. Evidently under Fairfax's influence, on 16 November the Council sent its own constitutional proposals to Charles at Newport. These were similar to the *Heads of the Proposals* which the King had rejected earlier, and provided for biennial parliaments elected on a new franchise and for their control over the armed forces and their right to appoint ministers and officials, thus diminishing the King's authority to an absolute minimum. Charles immediately rejected them, if indirectly, on 17 November. Next day a *Remonstrance* was drawn up by Commissary-General Ireton which highlighted the danger of negotiating any further with the King and put the case for bringing him to justice because he was personally responsible for launching the second civil war. This *Remonstrance* was approved by the Council of Officers and presented by an army delegation to the House of Commons on 2 November. The majority in the Commons postponed consideration of the *Remonstrance* because it believed that a treaty with the King could still be concluded.

The postponement provoked the Council of Officers now meeting at St Albans under General Fairfax, while Cromwell, outside Pontefract Castle, started writing to Colonel Hammond to suggest to him that the army was 'a lawful power' entitled to take action against 'this man against whom the Lord

Opening page of a pamphlet written by Captain Edward Cooke, an officer who became friendly with Charles I when he was a prisoner in the Isle of Wight and took part in a conference at Newport, the island's capital, during 1648. After the conference Cooke tried to help the King escape from his confinement on the island

had witnessed'. However, Hammond maintained that it was his duty to obey Parliament and not the army. On 21 November, six days before the Parliamentary commissioners left the Isle of Wight, Fairfax summoned Hammond to army headquarters in order to remove his scruples, while Ireton wrote to Hammond telling him he must obey his military superiors. After he arrived on the mainland Hammond received instructions from Parliament to return to the Isle of Wight as Governor, but he was put under arrest by the army and taken to Windsor, where the military headquarters had been removed to, and other officers were sent to Newport with orders to conduct Charles back to Carisbrooke Castle.

Two of the King's Gentlemen of the Bedchamber (the Duke of Richmond and the 2nd Earl of Lindsey), who were with Charles at Newport, Captain Edward Cooke, a friendly officer in Hammond's regiment, and a Groom of the Bedchamber, Henry Firebrace by name, all begged Charles to escape at once; the night was dark and a kindly local merchant had a boat ready. But Charles retorted that if the attempt should miscarry 'it would exasperate the Army and dishearten his friends'.[14] So he refused his last opportunity to escape from the island before the officers despatched by Fairfax arrived to collect him and carry him by coach on the first stage of the route that led to his trial and execution. Charles was driven a little beyond Yarmouth harbour on the north-west coast of the island, where after an hour's stay he embarked – 'a sorrowful spectacle', as one of his attendants, Sir Thomas Herbert, recalled, 'and a great example of fortune's inconstancy'[15] – to cross the sea on a three-hour passage to Hurst Castle in Hampshire, which had been erected as a blockhouse by King Henry VIII. There, Herbert's account continues, 'on both sides the sea beats, so as at spring-tides and in stormy weather the land passage is formidable and hazardous'. In 'this wretched place', where the air was noxious and the rooms had to be lit by candles even at midday, Charles was confined while momentous events were taking place in London.

13 The Trial and Execution of Charles I

During the last months of 1648 the contest of wills between the leaders of the army which won the second civil war and the majority in the House of Commons reached its climax. As has been noticed, a week before the Parliamentarian commissioners who had been negotiating with the King at Newport left the Isle of Wight the army presented its *Remonstrance* to Parliament demanding that 'this evil and dangerous treaty' should be broken off and that 'the capital and great author of our troubles should be brought to justice'.[1] The army's chief protagonist remained the austere Henry Ireton, for his father-in-law, Oliver Cromwell, was lingering in the north of England after returning from Scotland. General Thomas Fairfax, however, had endorsed the submission of the *Remonstrance* to the House of Commons apparently on the presumption that if it were accepted and King Charles was put on trial he would be deposed, not punished by death.

In the House of Commons, on the other hand, expectations that the King's concessions at Newport would bear fruit in a constitutional settlement were still high. During the second civil war, mainly because Cromwell and other army officers who were members of parliament had been absent on campaign, the Presbyterians still headed by Holles and moderates who genuinely sought a peace treaty with the King were in control of the House of Commons. So on the day before Charles was removed from the Isle of Wight to Hurst Castle the Commons rejected the army's *Remonstrance* by 123 votes to 53.

Ireton now determined that the army should march up to London and compel the House of Commons to dissolve itself in order to be replaced by 'a just Representative'.[2] The army duly entered London on 2 December and General Fairfax set up his headquarters in Whitehall Palace. When the Commons met on 4 December they were informed by the army that the King had been forcibly removed from Carisbrooke to Hurst Castle. Next day they voted that Charles had been removed without their knowledge or consent. Furthermore, later in the day they defiantly voted, though by a relatively small majority (129 to 83), that the King's answers at Newport were 'a ground for the course to proceed for a settlement of the peace of the kingdom'. After the House rose Henry Ireton, Thomas Harrison and other leading officers, together with a few members of parliament who were opposed to any agreement with the King, gathered in a conference near Whitehall and resolved forcibly to purge the House of Commons of those members who still wanted to come to terms with Charles, thus overruling Ireton, who would have preferred a complete dissolution followed by the presentation of an invitation to trusted radical members to act in an advisory capacity to the governing army until new elections could be held. During that evening lists were drawn up of the members who were to be excluded, leaving enough to carry on the normal duties of the House. General Fairfax was not consulted about the proposed purge, but was merely notified by Ireton what was going to be done in his name.[3] Next day (Wednesday 6 December) soldiers belonging to the New Model army surrounded the House of Commons, sent away the City's trained bands which usually guarded the Parliament buildings, and when the members of the Commons arrived as was customary at eight o'clock in the morning Colonel Thomas Pride, who had been given the list of members condemned to be excluded from the House by the army, took charge of the proceedings.

On 6 and 7 December over a hundred members were arrested or secluded. About another 160 members later withdrew in protest. Altogether the Purge resulted in about three-fifths of the members eligible to sit ceasing to attend the debates and left only fifty or sixty prepared to do so. In effect the government of the country was now in the hands of the Council of Officers headed by Henry Ireton and joined by Oliver Cromwell, who arrived from the north of England on the evening of the Purge; he gave it his approval, though it is conceivable that like Ireton he would have preferred a complete dissolution of this Parliament, which, in fact, he was to carry out four years later.[4]

Charles stayed in Hurst Castle until 19 December. While he was there he was still optimistic about his future. He told his captors that there was no law by which he could be tried and that if the army should threaten his life the London city magistrates, foreign princes and the Royalists in Ireland might intervene on his behalf.[5] When he was still in the castle Colonel Thomas Harrison arrived there to arrange his removal, though Charles did not see him then; but he was delighted to learn from the Governor that he was to be taken to Windsor Castle, where he arrived on 23 December. On his way there he met Colonel Harrison, who, as always, was handsomely dressed, wearing a velvet peaked hat, a new buff coat, and a richly fringed crimson scarf about his waist. The King spoke to him

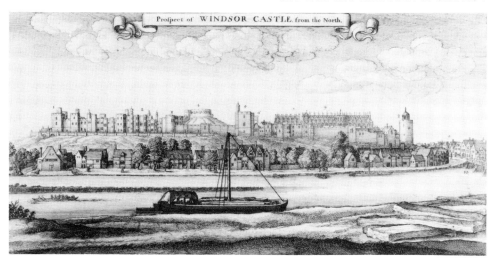

Windsor Castle: an engraving by Hollar

about a rumour he had heard that the Colonel had been involved in a plot to murder him. Harrison indignantly denied this, but said 'the law was equally obliging to great and small and that 'justice had no respect to persons'.[6] Once in Windsor Castle the King maintained his health by walking on the long terrace and his spirits by constantly praying. The Duke of Hamilton, who had been captured after the Preston campaign, was also a prisoner in the castle. While Charles was there Oliver Cromwell came to the castle in an attempt to collect evidence from Hamilton that Charles had invited the Scottish Engagers to invade England during the second civil war, but Hamilton refused to incriminate the King. Neither Cromwell nor anyone else from the army or any of the army's political associates saw the King while he was at Windsor. He was kept there, in the end deprived of the usual ceremonies of royal state until after his trial for treason began.

The purged House of Commons, now little more than the tool of the army, had on 23 December appointed a committee on which two avid republicans, Henry Marten and Thomas Scot, were dominant, to draw up proposals for the trial. The committee was later enlarged to include Cromwell and other officers who were members of the attenuated Commons. It reported on 2 January 1649 and presented a draft ordinance which was passed without a division. In it 'Charles Stuart, the now King of England' was accused of 'a wicked design . . . to introduce arbitrary and tyrannical government' and in pursuit of that aim had 'levied and maintained a cruel war in the land against the Parliament and kingdom'. He was therefore to be put on trial before a special court consisting of 150 commissioners. The quorum in the Commons since Pride's Purge had been reduced to forty and usually the attendance was about fifty out of a nominal 471.[7] The ordinance was agreed to and sent up to the House of Lords, twelve members in total, which rejected it chiefly on the ground that the King could not be condemned for treason against himself. On 3 January the Commons therefore amended the ordinance, which it rechristened an Act of Parliament, and declared that the Commons 'representing the people' had 'the supreme power in the nation', and removed from it the names of the peers who had been appointed as commissioners in the first draft. Instead of 150 commissioners 135 were nominated to act in the High Court of Justice as both judges and jurors.

The High Court duly met for the first time on 8 January in the Painted Chamber, a room in the Palace of Westminster, which lay south of Westminster Hall where the public trial was to be held. It was draped with standards captured during the civil war including those at Naseby. Here fifty-three commissioners including Fairfax, Cromwell, Ireton, Harrison, Pride and John Okey, all of whom fought at Naseby, were present. Fairfax had evidently not realized until then that the intention was to try the King for his life; he did not attend any further meetings of the High Court and eleven years later was to play an important part in restoring the King's son as Charles II to the throne of his ancestors. Oliver Cromwell, on the other hand, was determined actively to ensure that the trial should be conducted with some plausible appearance of legality and justice.[8] That was why he attempted, before the Act establishing the Court was passed, to secure the support of the two most distinguished lawyers in the country, Bulstrode Whitelocke and Thomas Widdrington, Keepers of the Great Seal, and to persuade them to sanction the trial and induce them to gain the approval of members of parliament who had voluntarily ceased to attend the House of Commons after Pride's Purge. Neither of these lawyers nor three chief justices nor William Lenthall, who was Master of the Rolls as well as Speaker of the House of Commons, would have anything to do with the trial. One of the chief justices, Oliver St John, was a kinsman and friend of Cromwell. John Selden, the most learned lawyer in the Commons, also refused to lend his presence to the trial; nor would Sir Henry Vane. the Younger, once Oliver's closest friend. Major-General Philip Skippon, who commanded the Parliamentarian infantry at the battle of Naseby, also refused to act as a commissioner. Plainly, whatever these men thought about Charles's behaviour none of them believed that the Court had any historical validity or moral justification.

After a further meeting in the Painted Chamber on the afternoon of Saturday 20 January the King's trial opened publicly at around two o'clock in Westminster Hall.[9] The delay of nearly a fortnight since the High Court first assembled was caused by the need to clear and prepare the Hall and to agree on the terms of the indictment. King Charles had been brought to St James's Palace from Windsor

Castle by coach and then to Whitehall whence he was taken by barge along the Thames and placed in a house that had belonged to the antiquarian, Sir Robert Cotton. The officers and their republican friends who organized the trial had only with difficulty found a qualified judge, John Bradshaw, to preside over it. Bradshaw was at times unconvincingly argumentative and at other times firm. The chief prosecutor was John Cook, the Solicitor-General, who was both a religious fanatic and a devoted republican. The president, prosecuting attorneys, commissioners and the prisoner were given seats at the south end of the Hall while the spectators were accommodated in the main body of the Hall separated from the participants by barriers. The King was brought in early in the afternoon. After Cook had read out the charge that he was 'a Tyrant, Traitor, Murderer and a public and implacable enemy to the Commonwealth of England' and 'had maliciously levied war against the present Parliament and the people therein represented' Charles naturally demanded to know by what lawful authority he was being tried. Bradshaw replied, as had been agreed beforehand, that the authority was 'the People of England, of which he was the Elected King'. Charles retorted that England had never been an elective kingdom and that he had been chosen by God to govern, being entrusted by Him with the care of the liberties of the people. Bradshaw would not allow the King to complete his speech, ceased to argue with him, and ordered his removal from the Hall.

After a consultation in the Painted Chamber on the Monday morning sixty-two of the commissioners agreed that Bradshaw should again inform the King that the Court was established by the Commons of England assembled in Parliament and told that if he again refused to accept its authority and would not plead his case he would be treated as guilty and sentenced. On the Monday and Tuesday afternoons Bradshaw therefore reasserted the Court's authority derived from the purged House of Commons while the King denied it, but asked to speak for 'the liberties of the people of England'. Once more Bradshaw tried to interrupt him and finally ordered his removal by his guards.

Following the departure of the King from Westminster Hall the commissioners adjourned to the Painted Chamber where a compromise was adopted. A committee was appointed to meet there next day to hear witnesses in order to obtain proof that the King had personally started and waged war against Parliament. Among the witnesses were William James, a husbandman aged twenty-two, who described how he had seen the King marching at the head of his army towards Naseby field from Market Harborough and had asked the regiment commanded by Colonel St George (who had, in fact, been killed at the siege of Leicester before the battle) whether it would fight for him; David Evans, a smith aged twenty-three, also said that he had seen the King marching at the head of his army before the fight at Naseby; and Diogenes Edwards, a butcher aged twenty-one, said he had seen the King an hour and a half before the fight at Naseby and a mile and a half from the battlefield and afterwards seen 'many slain in the said battle'.[10]

These depositions, for what they were worth, were read out at a public session of the High Court on 25 January. Next day the High Court met privately in the Painted Chamber and decided that the King should be sentenced to death because of the depositions of the witnesses against him and his refusal to plead. After a further meeting on the morning of Saturday 27 January the Lord President, clad in a scarlet robe, and sixty-seven commissioners assembled in Westminster Hall during the afternoon to hear the sentence read. Charles asked permission to speak before the judgment was delivered. When he was allowed to do so he requested if he could speak not for his own particular case but on behalf of 'the Peace of the Kingdom and the Liberty of the Subject before the Lords and Commons in the Painted Chamber'. Bradshaw answered that he would refer this appeal privately to the members of the Court and let him know its decision within half an hour. When Bradshaw returned from the Court of Wards where the matter was discussed and Charles was brought back to Westminster Hall the President told the King it had been decided unanimously that no further delay would be tolerated and he must hear his sentence.

Though Charles warned him that he would have to answer for this decision 'at the dreadful day of Judgment', Bradshaw was unperturbed and proceeded to deliver a lengthy, carefully prepared speech in which he attempted to provide legal and historical justification for the authority of the Court, maintaining that the Parliament of England provided 'the sole Makers of the Law', that 'the Law

A facsimile of the King's death-warrant. Cromwell's and Ireton's signatures appear in the first and second columns respectively

was his Master', and that the great bulwark of the liberties of the people was the Parliament which he had tried 'to subvert and rout up'. The clerk of the court then read the charges drawn up on parchment. As Charles had refused to answer the charges Bradshaw pronounced the King guilty and the clerk read out the sentence: 'the said Charles Stuart as a Tyrant, Traitor, Murderer and a public Enemy, shall be put to death, by the severing of his Head from his Body'. The King was not allowed to speak again after the sentence was read out, but was forcibly removed by the guards and carried to Whitehall in a sedan chair.

One fact about the trial and sentencing which is noteworthy is that no evidence was furnished to prove that the King had been responsible for the invasion of England by the Scottish Engagers. Oliver Cromwell, who was anxious to justify the case against Charles beyond any possible doubt, had seen the Duke of Hamilton two or three times in Windsor Castle in a vain attempt to extract testimony from him. Although he must have known that the leaders of the Engagers had visited Charles both at Hampton Court and Carisbrooke Castle the Engagement had never been published in England. Scottish commissioners came to London from Edinburgh at the beginning of January to protest

A contemporary German engraving of the execution of King Charles I in front of the Banqueting House in Whitehall palace on the afternoon of 30 January 1649

against trying the King for his life. After all he was King of Scotland as well as of England. Even the Marquis of Argyll, who as late as October 1648 had been a close ally of Cromwell against the Engagers, summoned the Scottish Parliament to meet on 4 January 1649 to condemn the trial of a native Scottish King.[11]

On 28 January Charles was brought back to St James's Palace where he was accompanied by Dr William Juxon, the former Bishop of London, who had volunteered to stay with him until the end, sharing his captivity. He alone was with Charles on the scaffold which was erected in front of the Banqueting House in Whitehall Palace. The day before he died Charles was permitted to see his youngest children, Princess Elizabeth and Henry, Duke of Gloucester. He gave them jewels and told them he had forgiven all his enemies before retiring early. On the morning of 30 January he walked across St James's Park to Whitehall Palace and that afternoon stepped out from a window of the Banqueting House on to the scaffold. There he delivered his final speech, though few heard it. He protested that he had not begun the war against the Houses of Parliament and stated that he died a Christian according to the tenets of the Church of England. His last words were: 'I go from a Corruptible to an Incorruptible Crown where no disturbance can be but Peace and Joy for evermore'. The execution took place at about two o'clock. On 9 February his body, with the head sewn back on to it, was buried in a grave in St George's Chapel at Windsor Castle 'without any words or other ceremony than the tears and sighs of the few beholders'.[12]

On the same day as the burial the third issue of the first edition of the book called *Eikon Basilike – The Pourtraiture of His Sacred Majesty in His Solitudes and Sufferings* was published, a book which had been based on a core of material that the King had composed and finally approved when he was in the Isle of Wight. Dr John Gauden, who subsequently became Bishop of Exeter and had actually written the book, was to tell the Earl of Clarendon after Charles II returned to London as King in 1660 when it came out: 'What preparations it made in all men's minds for the happy restoration . . . In a word it was an army and did vanquish more than any sword could'.[13] Unquestionably Charles I's martyrdom did more to secure the future of the English monarchy than if he had won the battle of Naseby.

CONCLUSION

Although it has been questioned, little doubt can remain that Charles I was, after his own fashion, a true Christian. He was 'a man of prayer, an ardent and simple faith and a great strictness of life'.[1] The Almighty, he believed, had chosen him to reign and rule over the English people more completely than his ancestors had ever done in Scotland, and it was his duty to care for them as a loving father. He accepted the hierarchical concept of society. The bishops, he thought, were essential to the maintenance of the monarchy, the Church being even more important to it than the armed forces, for, as he assured his wife, 'if the pulpits teach not obedience the King will have small comfort from the militia'. He told his son: 'As the Church can never flourish without the protection of the Crown, so the dependency of the Church upon the Crown is the chiefest support of regal authority'. He also denied that his earnestness in fighting for the Elizabethan Church of England arose purely out of party policy or for reasons of State. The bishops, he insisted, were the successors of the twelve apostles and of those approved in St Paul's Epistles to Timothy and Titus.[2] Were he to consent to their abolition it would be 'a sin of the highest nature' and a violation of his conscience. Though not only his Queen but several of his courtiers and even one or two bishops themselves urged him to be less intransigent on the matter so long as he could retain his throne, he stressed, on the contrary, that to safeguard the episcopacy was his moral duty; and on reflection even his approval of the exclusion of the bishops from the House of Lords, as he had done before the civil war began, had been sinful and a decision for which he had been 'justly punished'.[3] His extreme devotion to the bishops was certainly out of tune with the feelings of the majority of his subjects.

Yet while Charles was ultimately inflexible on the future of the Church, to attain his political and military ends he was unscrupulous and capable of trickery or 'subtle' and 'cunning', as his wife more politely put it.[4] For example, both when he was at Hampton Court and on the Isle of Wight he gave his word of honour not to escape from his imprisonment and yet made every effort to do so. He lied about his promises to the Irish Catholics, he gave diametrically opposite promises to the Presbyterians and Independents and to the Scots and the Irish, and in negotiating with Parliament he offered concessions he had no intention of fulfilling. He was, in fact, in many ways high-minded, but often deliberately deceitful. He was convinced that any devious means of regaining his power, other than by war, was justifiable because he believed that it was his divine obligation to ensure the welfare of his subjects, a sacred trust conferred on him by God. It has been argued that he was no more deceitful than most politicians,[5] but, after all, Oliver Cromwell, having vainly tried to treat with him, came to the conclusion that Charles was 'so great a dissembler and so false a man that he was not to be trusted' and that was an opinion that cost the King his life.

There has been much debate about whether Charles was firm in his character or subject to persuasion by the last person to whom he had spoken or written. Veronica Wedgwood, for instance, thought he held his opinions with great firmness and also referred to his 'inconvenient obstinacy',[6] while other historians have remarked on his hesitations and changes of mind. Both Henriette Marie and Edward Hyde, who knew him intimately, considered that he lacked firmness. The Queen warned him against his lack of perseverance and told him that it was 'better to follow out a bad resolution than to change it so often'.[7] Hyde wrote that while he had 'an excellent understanding he was not confident enough of it; which made him oftentimes change his own opinion for a worse and follow the advice of a man that did not judge as well as himself'.[8] But no doubt the fact was that, like most men in high positions, he was utterly determined on some questions and entirely flexible on others. Indeed, he remarked: 'I am blamed for granting too much and yet not yielding enough'.[9] Certainly he had his principles, which he was most reluctant to betray. After his defeat at Naseby he told Sir Edward Nicholas:

> I resolve (by the grace of God) never to yield up the Church to the government of Papists, Presbyterians or Independents, nor to injure my successors by lessening the Crown of the ecclesiastical and military power which my predecessors left me or forsake my friends, much less let them suffer when I do not for their faithfulness to me.[10]

Another facet of Charles's character was his genuine reluctance to injure his subjects unnecessarily. Sir Edward Walker wrote of his 'wonted clemency' and Charles himself wrote: 'I never had any victory which was without sorrow because it was on my own subjects'.[11] He had, Clarendon noted, 'a tenderness and compassion of nature which restrained him from ever doing a hard-hearted thing'. So because of 'the lenity of his nature and the tenderness of his conscience, in all cases of blood they made him choose the softer way'.[12] Therefore, he disliked storming cities and allowing plunder. But wars cannot be fought in kid gloves; and that surely was one of the main reasons why he lost the first civil war.

Moreover, he lacked confidence in himself; and it has been argued that his

Charles I, a pencil drawing by Sir Robert Strange after Van Dyck

'sense of personal inadequacy explains his assertion of authority over trifles'.[13] This lack of self-confidence, his tendency to be irresolute, and his clemency were all reflected in the decisions he took during the civil war. After the battle of Edgehill he rejected the advice to dispatch immediately a flying column to attack London; yet later when the Earl of Essex had brought his army back safely from the battlefield he gave his own army a belated order to advance upon the capital. Because he was upset by the losses sustained in capturing Bristol he refused to storm Gloucester. Though he promised Rupert to maintain a defensive position in the Oxford area during 1644 after the Prince left for the north he did not do so and was forced to leave his base, but afterwards admitted that he ought to have followed Rupert's advice. After his victory at Lostwithiel in Cornwall in the same year he failed to exploit it, leaving the Roundhead garrisons in the south-west intact. Equally he rejected Rupert's counsel to resume the battle against the disintegrated Parliamentarian forces at Newbury towards the end of the year. Before the battle of Naseby he sent confusing orders to his generals in the south-west and, having unwisely divided his army into two parts, he overruled Rupert and other experienced officers in his Council of War and determined to fight a battle with inferior strength, apparently because his courtiers persuaded him that the New Model Army was untried and vulnerable. The word 'wilfulness' was frequently applied to his decisions.

Another of Charles's pronounced characteristics was his unfailing optimism and this was exemplified in military matters. In spite of the dismal failure of the first combined operation launched against the Spaniards at the beginning of his reign he twice allowed the Duke of Buckingham to resume the unprovoked war against them and against the French as well. Although Prince Rupert was comprehensively beaten at the battle of Marston Moor, he afterwards appointed him as his Chief of Staff. At the outset of 1645 he assured his wife that he was 'in a better condition this year than I have been since the rebellion began'. Four days after the defeat at Naseby he asserted that he was confident that: '. . . my late loss would soon be forgotten and likewise it may (by the grace of God) put such a turn in my affairs as to make me in a far better condition than I have ever been in at any time since the rebellion began'. When he was making up his mind to leave Oxford at the beginning of 1646 he assured his wife that the root of the monarchy was left entire and 'it will spring up again as fair as ever' and even when he was a prisoner of the Scottish Covenanters at Newcastle upon Tyne at the end of the year he told her that he was 'confident [that] within a very small time I shall be recalled with much honour'.[14] Though he was afterwards offered reasonable terms for a settlement by the army leaders he informed them that they could not do without him.

It was only after the army took him away from the Isle of Wight at the beginning of 1649 that he at last realized that he was in a perilous situation. Yet even during the trial for his life he still thought if he were allowed to address the two Houses of Parliament he could convince them of his case 'on behalf of the kingdom and the liberty of the subject'. That Charles's defeat at the battle of Naseby and his subsequent misfortunes were largely owing to the weaknesses in his character can hardly be questioned. That does not mean that he was an unintelligent man, that he did not listen to the advice he was given, or that he was an insincere Christian, let alone that he was paranoid. But if one contrasts his character with that of his father or his eldest son, one has to conclude that it was his own mistakes that cost him his throne and his life.

APPENDIX A: THE STRENGTH OF THE ARMIES AT NASEBY

No agreement exists among academic historians or historical authors on the precise size of the armies that fought in the battle of Naseby. Colonel Rogers and Professor Kenyon agree with S.R. Gardiner, who published his chapter on Naseby as long ago as 1889, in the revised estimate of the size of the Royalist army which, after he consulted Colonel W.G. Ross, he put at 7,400; this he believed to be little more than half the size of the Parliamentarian army.[1] A.H. Burne, writing in *The Battlefields of England* (1950) also roughly accepted the same figure. But curiously enough. W.G. Ross, discussing the question in vol. III of the *English Historical Review* of 1888, quoted 'three intelligencers' as saying the Royalists amounted to about 12,000 men.

Rogers and Kenyon differ over the strength of the Parliamentarians: Rogers says 15,000, Kenyon about 12,850. William Seymour in *Decisive Factors in Twenty Great Battles of the World* (1988) gives the Royalists as 8,180 men (4,280 cavalry and 3,900 infantry) facing 14,600 under Fairfax (7,200 cavalry, 6,400 infantry and 1,000 dragoons). Professor Woolrych puts the Royalists at 9,000 (half cavalry and half infantry) and the Parliamentarians at 14,000. The late Brigadier Peter Young, writing in 1985, made the Royalists about 9,200, but he estimated the size of the cavalry differently on different pages: on p. 37 of his book on *Naseby 1645* he puts the cavalry at 5,590, but on p. 237 his total comes to 5,080. A higher estimate of the Royalists can be found in Clement Markham's biography of Fairfax: this was 10,820 (5,520 cavalry and 5,300 infantry); however, he counts the Newark cavalry (800 men) twice over, once on the left wing and once in the reserve. R.N. Dore writing on 'Sir William Brereton's Siege of Chester and the Campaign of Naseby' was of the opinion that 'Charles fought Naseby with an army no bigger than the one he had set out from Oxford', i.e. 11,000.[2] His estimate for Fairfax's army was 13,600. Thus, whereas there is rough agreement among historians that the Parliamentarian army contained between 13,000 and 16,000 men, the size of the Royalist army ranges between 7,400 and 11,000.

Turning to the contemporary sources, the lowest estimate is founded ultimately in Clarendon's *History of the Rebellion*. But Clarendon was nowhere near the battle when it took place and derived his account of it from Sir Edward

Walker, who wrote his brief account in Paris during February 1647. This does not include a total figure, but merely states that Rupert on the right wing had about 2,000 men, while 'the main body of foot', led by Lord Astley, consisted of 2,500 with about 1,300 in the reserve.[3] No figure is given for the left wing. Joshua Sprigge, who examined the evidence fairly soon after the battle, wrote: 'The battle was fought much upon equal advantage whether you respect the number on each side there being not five hundred odds on either side.' Bustrode Whitelocke wrote the same in his *Memorials*: 'The battle was exceeding bloody, both armies being very courageous and numerous and not five hundred odds on either side.' Presumably since the *Memorials* were not published until 1682 Whitelocke lifted this from Sprigge.[4]

In the map drawn by Sir Bernard de Gomme, now in the British Library, it is specifically stated that the Royalist army consisted of 4,000 foot and 3,500 horse. This is the most powerful evidence for the low figure accepted by a majority of modern historians. But in the same collection there is a map drawn by de Gomme of the battle of Marston Moor in which he wrote that the Royalist army consisted of 17,000 men (11,000 foot and 6,000 horse) whereas, in fact, the army's total strength at that battle was only 14,000; the number of cannon employed in the battle which he gives is also incorrect. Peter Newman, who had analysed that battle in depth rightly says that de Gomme's map needs to be treated with caution and the same must apply to his map of Naseby.[5]

Another reason for accepting a low estimate of the size of the Royalist army is that although it is known to have consisted of some 5,300 infantry and 5,520 cavalry before the storming of Leicester[6] on 30 May because of losses during the siege of the city and the need to supply a garrison afterwards it was materially reduced in strength. Indeed, Charles wrote to Sir Edward Nicholas on 4 June, soon after the siege was over, 'my army is so weak being not 4,000 foot and 3,500 horse'.[7] However, after this, as he wrote in the same letter his intention was to 'gather up stragglers' while two days earlier Sir Samuel Luke had written that the King's strength was 4,000 foot and 7,000 horse 'if fame be not a liar'.[8] No doubt fame was a liar, but at least the Parliamentarians did not imagine Charles's army was 'weak'.

There are various contemporary estimates of the size of the army under Fairfax mainly derived from the letters of Luke. On 3 May 1645 he estimated that it consisted of 22,000, roughly the establishment strength of the New Model Army; on 9 June he told Major Gilbert Carr that 'the number is 8,000 horse and 7,000 foot'.[9] One day before the battle he told the Earl of Essex that the army 'cannot be less than 8,000 horse and 7,000 foot'.[10] Barry Denton, calculating the size of the horse from the number of cornets identified (sixty) estimates the total strength of the Parliamentarian cavalry at 6,000 and the infantry, assuming it was near establishment strength, at 9,600:[11] this is 1,000 higher than Brigadier Peter Young's estimate. Lord Belasyse's estimate in retrospect was 15,000.[12] As this coincides with Luke's final estimate on the day before the battle, after he had inspected Fairfax's army, it seems reasonable.

To return to the Royalist army, another way of measuring its size is this: 5,000 prisoners out of the Royalist infantry were captured in the battle, 4,500 of whom Fiennes led up to London.[13] According to a report made by two Parliamentary commissioners residing with the army to the Speaker of the House of Commons dated on the day of the battle 600 infantrymen had been killed; and 200 cavalrymen were also stated to have been killed in the fighting.[14] Others were killed in the pursuit. In addition some of the foot soldiers must have got away from the battlefield. The bulk of the Royalist cavalry fled and escaped to Leicester: these are estimated to have numbered 4,000 (possibly more) and to have been almost intact.[15] Suppose therefore that 5,000 prisoners were taken, 1,000 were killed and 4,000 escaped, the Royalist army would have numbered at least 10,000. It is, therefore, possible to credit the recollection of Lord Belasyse, who after all attended the Council of War and took part in the battle, that the Royalists had 'not exceeding 12,000 horse and foot' – perhaps between 10,500 and 11,000. This, incidentally, was Gardiner's original estimate.[16]

APPENDIX B: BIBLIOGRAPHICAL ESSAY

The principal authority for the battle of Naseby on the Parliamentarian side is the account written by Joshua Sprigge entitled *Anglia Rediviva; England's Recovery: being the History of the Motions, Actions and Successes of the Army under the Immediate Conduct of his Excellency Sir Thomas Fairfax, Kt.*, first published in 1647 and reprinted in 1854. Although Sprigge appears to have been an army chaplain, there is no reason to suppose he was present at the battle. Sir Charles Firth wrote that his account contains little information that could have been derived from his own recollections, but it is 'a very judicious and accurate compilation' and contains a valuable map of the battle. John Okey, who commanded the dragoon regiment in the New Model Army during the battle, left an account entitled *A more particular and exact Relation* (Thomason tracts E 288 28) of his part in the battle.

On the Royalist side the most valuable account is by Sir Edward Walker, who was undoubtedly an eyewitness of the battle: his short description of it intended for the use of the Earl of Clarendon was written in Paris in 1647 and was included in his *Historical Discourses upon Several Occasions* (1705). There is also a brief report by Richard Symonds, a captain in the King's Lifeguard which fought at Naseby, in his *Diary*, published by the Camden Society in 1859. Colonel Sir Henry Slingsby, who also fought in the battle, evidently as a cavalry officer, and Colonel John Belasyse, who served as a volunteer in the King's reserve at the battle, also left short but important descriptions of the battle. The Earl of Clarendon's account of the battle was based on Walker, but he may have had other sources of information. Thus, surprisingly, there is more authentic information about the battle from the Royalist than from the Parliamentarian side.

The most valuable secondary book on the battle is Peter Young's *Naseby 1645* (1985). It contains a detailed analysis of all the regiments that took part in the battle and it reprints the texts of most of the original authorities, including the letters written about it by General Fairfax, Lieutenant-General Cromwell and the Parliamentary commissioners, Leighton and Herbert. But unfortunately Brigadier Young's own description of the battle, though containing one or two *obiter dicta*, is unsatisfactory; moreover, his publisher refused to include illustrations or maps in the book except for one map which was drawn for the author by a friend of his and is therefore imaginative. A fuller account is to be found in Peter Young and Richard Holmes, *The English Civil War* (1974), ch. 18, p. 238 *seq.* The latest secondary account of the battle is Barry Denton, *Naseby Fight*, published by the Partisan Press in 1988 and three times re-issued with minor additions. There is an excellent chapter on the battle in Austin Woolrych, *Battles of the English Civil War* (1961), with maps, illustrations and bibliography. Recent short pieces on the battle are a booklet by Sir Charles Rowley, *The Battle of Naseby 1645*, which contains useful maps, but was severely criticized by Nigel Jackson in *English Civil War notes and queries*, no. 39, published by Caliver Books, and *The Campaign of Naseby 1645* by Stuart A. Asquith (Osprey Publishing, 1979), containing elaborate coloured illustrations. There are also a few not entirely accurate pages in John Kenyon, *The Civil Wars in England* (1988), pp. 143–7. Professor Kenyon's book is an important addition to the books by Peter Young and Ronald Hutton on the organization of the rival armies.

No entirely satisfactory biography of King Charles I or analysis of his military strategy has yet been published – a remarkable fact – nor is there an edition of his surviving letters, such as Thomas Carlyle initiated for Oliver Cromwell. (Dr Morrill has recently written an illuminating article 'Textualizing and Contextualizing Cromwell' in the *Historical Journal*, vol. 33, 1990.) The best biography of Charles to date is by Pauline Gregg, *King Charles I* (1981), though it deals only briefly with his campaigns and battles; but there are several illuminating views about his character in, for example, Richard Ollard, *The Image of a King* (1979), C.V. Wedgwood, *The King's Peace* and *The King's War* (1955 and 1958) and Conrad Russell, *The Causes of the English Civil War* (1990), ch. 8, 'The Man Charles Stuart'.

To my mind one of the best writings on his character is to be found in *King Charles I*, Historical Association pamphlet no. 11. Charles's military strategy and tactics are discussed in Peter Young's books and in Young and Holmes, *op. cit.* Charles's proclamations have been published in two volumes (ed. J.F. Larkin, 1983) and there is a useful list of where his letters, speeches and writings can be found in Gregg, pp. 464–5. By far the most illuminating of his letters are those edited and published by J. Bruce in *Charles I in 1646* (Camden Society 1856); some of his correspondence with his Queen before the battle of Naseby is in the House of Lords MSS. The letters he wrote to Jane Whorwood when he was in prison in the Isle of Wight are also fascinating: see C.W. Firebrace, *Honest Harry: biography of Sir Henry Firebrace* (1932) and Maurice Ashley, *Charles I and Oliver Cromwell* (1987), ch. 4.

Books on the origins and general character of the civil wars are too numerous to be detailed and are constantly being updated: my own book *The English Civil War* (revised 1990) is among them. I should like to express my gratitude to Sir Charles Rowley (who showed me round the battlefield of Naseby), Professor Austin Woolrych and Dr John Morrill for the advice they have generously given me in writing the present book.

NOTES

List of Abbreviations

Abbott	W.C. Abbott (ed.), *The Writings and Speeches of Oliver Cromwell* (1937–47)
Bruce	J. Bruce (ed.), *Charles I in 1646* (Camden Society 1856)
Clarendon	Edward Earl of Clarendon, *The History of the Rebellion and Civil Wars in England* (ed. W. Dunn Macray, 1888)
CSP (Dom)	*Calendar of State Papers (Domestic)*
Gardiner	S.R. Gardiner, *History of the Great Civil War 1642–1649* (1891–93)
Gregg	Pauline Gregg, *King Charles I* (1981)
Hutton	Ronald Hutton, *The Royalist War Effort 1642–1646* (1982)
Sprigge	Joshua Sprigge, *Anglia Rediviva; England's Recovery* (1854)
Walker	Sir Edward Walker, *Historical Discourses upon Several Occasions* (1705)
Young	Peter Young, *Naseby 1645* (1985)

Introduction

1. A.H. Burne, *The Battlefields of England* (1950), p. 252.
2. P. Warwick, *Memoirs and Reflections upon the Reign of King Charles I*, p. 269.
3. *Cit.* J. Buchan, *Montrose* (1928), p. 88.
4. Charles to Henriette Marie from Oxford, 27 March 1645, Young, p. 328.
5. Hutton, p. 175.
6. Charles I to Nicholas from Daventry, *John Evelyn's Diary* (ed. H.B. Wheatley, 1879), pp. 145–50.
7. R. Bulstrode, *Memoirs and Reflections upon the Reign and Government of King Charles I and King Charles II* (1721), p. 125.
8. Warwick, *op. cit.*, p. 288.

1 King Charles and the Coming of the First Civil War

1. *Cit.* D. Harris Wilson, *King James VI and I* (1956), pp. 418, 422.
2. *Ibid.*, p. 248.
3. *Cit.* Derek Hirst, *Authority and Conflict* (1986), p. 117.
4. John Rushworth, *Historical Collections I* (1701), p. 447.
5. S.R. Gardiner, *The Constitutional Documents of the Puritan Revolution* (1906), pp. 66–70; Gregg, p. 173.
6. Clarendon, IV, p. 495; Bulstrode, *op. cit.*, pp. 184–5.
7. See in general Caroline Hibbard, *Charles I and the Popish Plot* (1983), p. 108 *seq.* But the influence of the Arminians has been exaggerated in the writings of Nicholas Tyache: see the criticisms of Peter White in *Past and Present* (1983 and 1985) and G.W. Bernard in *History*, 75, no. 244 (1990).
8. Gardiner, *op. cit.*, pp. 75–6.
9. Gregg, p. 186.
10. Gardiner, *op. cit.*, p. 115 *seq.*
11. David Underdown, *Revel, Riot and Rebellion* (1985), pp. 128–30.
12. Conrad Russell (ed.), *The Origins of the English Civil War* (1973), p. 27.
13. *The Private Journals of the Long Parliament* (1987), III.
14. John Fielding, 'Opposition to the Personal Rule of Charles I, the Diary of Robert Woodford 1637–1641', *Historical Journal* (1988), p. 783.
15. Conrad Russell, *The Causes of the English Civil War* (1990), pp. 11–12, citing Hamilton MSS. Professor Russell's extremely learned and highly technical book, *The Fall of the British Monarchies 1637–1642* (1991), did not appear until after the present book was completed. However, *The Causes of the English Civil War*, embodying the Ford lectures, was, Professor Russell states, 'an extended conclusion' to his latest book and much easier to read.
16. Cf. *ibid.*, p. 16, *seq*; but, of course, as Professor Russell observes, Charles had signed an Act against dissolving the Long Parliament without its own consent on 10 May 1641.
17. *Eikon Basilike* (ed. P.A. Knachel 1966), p. 17.

2 The Royalist Army

1. Hutton, p. 43.
2. J.L. Malcolm, *Caesar's Due: Loyalty and King Charles* (1983), p. 203.
3. M.D.G. Walklyn and Peter Young, 'A King in Search of his Soldiers', *Historical Journal* (1981), pp. 147–53.

4. This question is discussed in John Kenyon, *The Civil Wars in England* (1988), p. 37 *seq.*

5. Underdown, *op. cit.*, ch. 7.

6. *Calendar of State Papers (Venetian) 1642–1643*, p. 7.

7. P.R. Newman, 'The Royal Officer Corps 1642–1660', *Historical Journal*, no. 26, p. 945 *seq.* G.E. Aylmer has said: 'It has sometimes been suggested that younger sons had little to lose and so were readier to commit themselves on both sides in the civil war.' *Transactions of the Royal Historical Society*, no. 37, pp. 28–9.

8. R. Bulstrode, *op. cit.*, pp. 71, 115–16.

9. Ian Roy, 'The Royalist Council of War 1642–1646', *Bulletin of the Institute of Historical Research*, no. 35, p. 163 *seq.*

10. Clarendon, IV, pp. 490–1.

11. *Eikon Basilike*, pp. 38–9.

3 Charles and the Civil War till 1644

1. Charles I to James Marquis of Hamilton, 27 October 1642, G. Burnet, *The Memoirs of the Lives and Actions of James and William Dukes of Hamilton* (1677), p. 202.

2. Clarendon, II, p. 353.

3. Peter Young, *Edgehill 1642* (1967), p. 278.

4. Charles I to William Hamilton from Oxford, Burnet, *op. cit.*, p. 203.

5. Patrick Morrah, *Prince Rupert of the Rhine* (1976), p. 126.

6. Gregg, p. 383.

7. Charles to Rupert, E. Warburton, *Memoirs of Prince Rupert and the Cavaliers* (1849), II, pp. 415–16.

8. Waller to Committee of Both Kingdoms, *CSP (Dom)*, p. 233.

9. Margaret Toynbee and Peter Young, *Cropredy Bridge 1644* (1970), p. 73 *seq.*

10. Warburton, *op. cit.*, II, p. 438.

11. *Cit.* Mary Coate, *Cornwall in the Great Civil War and Interregnum* (1933), p. 140.

12. Walker, p. 131.

13. Gregg, p. 391.

4 The New Model Army

1. Sprigge, p. 7.
2. *Documents relating to the Quarrel between the Earl of Manchester and Oliver Cromwell* (1875), p. 71 *seq.*
3. *Camden Society Miscellany* (1883), VIII, p. 2.
4. Abbott, I, p. 314.
5. *House of Lords Journals*, VII, p. 226.
6. M.A. Kishlansky, *The Rise of the New Model Army* (1979), p. 49.
7. *Cit.* C.H. Firth, *Cromwell's Army* (1911), p. 47.
8. Sir Samuel Luke to Sir O. Luke, 10 June 1645, *Letter Books of Sir Samuel Luke* (ed. H.G. Tibbutt 1963), p. 311.
9. *Cit.* C.R. Markham, *A Life of the Great Lord Fairfax* (1870) from Fairfax's *Short Memorial*, p. 191, note 1.
10. Kishlansky, *op. cit.*, p. 74.

5 The Road to Naseby

1. Charles to Henriette Marie from Oxford 13 March 1645, J. Rushworth, *Historical Collections* (1701), V, p. 948.
2. Rupert to Legge from Ludlow, 18 March 1645, Warburton, *op.cit.*, III, pp. 63–4.
3. Charles to Henriette Marie from Oxford, 27 March 1645, *The King's Cabinet Opened* (1645), *cit.* Young, p. 328.
4. Sir Samuel Luke to Edward Massey, 3 May 1645, *Letter Books*, p. 266.
5. 'Proceedings of the New-Moulded Army' by Colonel Edward Wogan, *cit.* Young, p. 367.
6. Digby to Goring from Burton on Trent, 26 May 1645, Gardiner, II, p. 195.
7. Clarendon, IV, p. 7 *seq.*
8. P. Young and R. Holmes, *The English Civil War* (1974), p. 237.
9. J. Wilshere and S. Green, *The Siege of Leicester – 1645* (1984), p. 18.
10. Walker, p. 129.
11. Rupert to Legge from Daventry, 8 June 1645, Warburton, *op. cit.*, III, p. 100.
12. Charles to Henriette Marie from Daventry, 8 June 1645, Sprigge, p. 27.
13. Thomas Fairfax to Lord Fairfax from Marston, 4 June 1645, *Fairfax Correspondence* (1849), I, p. 279.

14. Luke to Committee of Both Kingdoms from Newport Pagnell, *Letter Books*, p. 307.
15. *Ibid.*, p. 319.
16. Richard Symonds, *Diary* (1859), p. 193.
17. Charles to Nicholas, *cit*. Gardiner, II, p. 207.
18. This is the view of Colonel Rogers and Barry Denton.
19. Sprigge, p. 37.
20. Walker, p. 131.
21. Sprigge, *loc. cit.*
22. Walker, *loc. cit.*

6 The Battle of Naseby – I

1. See Appendix A.
2. Walker, p. 130.
3. Austin Woolrych, *Battles of the English Civil War* (1961), p. 121, quoting 'W.G.', *A Just Apology for an Abused Army* (1647).
4. Sprigge, p. 38.
5. Sir Henry Slingsby's account, Young, p. 311.
6. Young, p. 65, states that Sir Horatio Crew from Somerset served in a regiment that fought at Cheriton and in the siege of Leicester which, according to Symonds, was 200 strong.
7. Walker, p. 131.
8. Young, p. 321.
9. Sprigge, p. 39.
10. This is Colonel Rogers's suggestion.
11. Young, pp. 336, 338.
12. Clarendon, IV, p. 44.

7 The Battle of Naseby – II

1. Young, p. 339.
2. *Ibid.*, p. 311.
3. Sprigge, pp. 41–2.
4. *Ibid.*, p. 41; Walker, p. 130.
5. Young, p. 339.
6. Sprigge, p. 41.
7. Young, p. 58.
8. Sprigge, p. 42.

9. *Ibid.*, p. 39.
10. *Ibid.*, pp. 39–40
11. *Ibid.*, p. 40.
12. Clarendon, IV, p. 45.
13. *Ibid.*
14. Young, p. 322.
15. *Ibid.*
16. Young, p. 339.
17. *Ibid.*, p. 322.
18. *Ibid.*, p. 335.
19. *Ibid.*, pp. 335–6.

8 The Battle of Naseby – III

1. Michael Roberts, *Essays in Swedish History* (1967), p. 90.
2. *CSP (Dom) 1645*, pp. 521–2.
3. Culpeper to Digby, 26 May 1645, Digby to Nicholas, 26 May 1645, *CSP (Dom)*, 1645, pp. 521–2; Charles to Henriette Marie, 8 June 1645, *cit. supra*, chapter 6, note 12.
4. Sprigge, p. 37.
5. H.C.B. Rogers, *Battles and Generals in the Civil War* (1968), p. 231.
6. Walker, p. 130.
7. Young, p. 338.
8. Walker, p. 130.
9. Young, p. 268.
10. Clarendon, IV, p. 46.
11. Account by Edward Wogan, who served in Okey's dragoons, Young, p. 368.
12. Walker, p. 131.
13. Sprigge, p. 47.
14. Markham, *op. cit.*, p. 221.
15. Austin Woolrych, 'Cromwell as a Soldier', *Oliver Cromwell and the English Revolution* (ed. John Morrill 1990), p. 104.

9 The Aftermath of Naseby

1. Sprigge, p. 51.
2. Rupert to Legge from Bewdley, 18 June 1645, Warburton, *op. cit.*, III, p. 119 *seq.*

3. Charles to Ormonde from Bewdley, 18 June 1645, C. Petrie, *The Letters, Speeches and Proclamations of King Charles I* (1935), p. 153.

4. *Ibid.*, p. 154.

5. Charles to Nicholas from Raglan, 6 July 1645, *Evelyn Memoirs* (ed. Wheatley 1906), 4, pp. 152–3.

6. *Cit.* C. Carlton, *Charles I: the Personal Monarch* (1983), p. 290.

7. Rupert to the Duke of Richmond from Bristol, 28 July 1645, Warburton, *op. cit.* III, p. 145.

8. Charles to Rupert from Cardiff, 3 August 1645, Clarendon, IV, p. 74. There are various slightly different versions of this letter.

9. Charles to the Prince of Wales from Brecknoch, 5 August 1645, *ibid.*, p. 78.

10. Gregg, p. 398.

11. Markham, *op. cit.*, p. 252.

12. P. Morrah, *Prince Rupert of the Rhine* (1976), p. 197.

13. Harleian MSS 4231 ff. 14–15, *cit.* Carlton, *op. cit.*, p. 295.

14. Clarendon, IV, p. 128.

10 The End of the First Civil War

1. Charles to Henriette Marie from Oxford, 4 January 1646, Bruce, p. 2.

2. Charles to Digby from Oxford, 20 March 1646, J.O. Halliwell-Phillips, *Letters of the Kings of England* (1846), II, pp. 402–3.

3. Charles to Henriette Marie from Oxford, 11 January 1646, Bruce, p. 7.

4. Gardiner, II, p. 317.

5. Charles to Henriette Marie from Oxford, 6 April 1646, Bruce, p. 32.

6. Charles to Henriette Marie, 22 April 1646, Bruce, p. 38.

7. Charles to Henriette Marie from Newcastle upon Tyne, 20 May 1646, Bruce, p. 40.

8. Charles to Henriette Marie, 21 November 1646, Halliwell-Phillips, *op. cit.*, II, p. 430.

9. Charles to Henriette Marie, 4 December 1646, Bruce, p. 100.

11 Charles the Prisoner

1. Sir Thomas Herbert's narrative, G.S. Stevenson, *Charles I in Captivity* (1927), p. 13.

2. Belliévre to Brienne, 22 February 1647, *Montreuil Correspondence*, II, 1645–8 (1899), p. 7.
3. Gardiner, III, p. 36.
4. Austin Woolrych, *Soldiers and Statesmen* (1987), p. 37.
5. *Ibid.*, p. 69 *seq.*
6. Stevenson, *op. cit.*, p. 55.
7. Valerie Pearl, 'London's Counter-Revolution', *The Interregnum, the Quest for a Settlement 1646–1660* (ed. G.E. Aylmer 1972), p. 35 *seq.*
8. Ian Gentles, 'The Struggle for London in the Second Civil War', *Historical Journal* (1963), p. 277 *seq.*
9. *Clarke Papers* (ed. C.H. Firth, 1891), I, p. 85.
10. 'Memoirs of Sir John Berkeley', J. Ashburnham, *Narrative on his Attendance on King Charles I*, II (1830), p. cliv.
11. Woolrych, *op. cit.*, p. 179.
12. Ashburnham II, p. clvii.
13. *Cit.* Woolrych, *op. cit.*, p. 183.
14. Ashburnham, II, p. 100.
15. Woolrych, *op. cit.*, pp. 264–8.
16. Ashburnham, II, clxiii; *House of Lords Journals*, IX, p. 519.
17. Ashburnham, II, p. 130.

12   The Second Civil War

1. Ashburnham, II, pp. 107 *seq*, clxiv *seq.*
2. Gardiner, III, pp. 257–8.
3. Belliévre to Brienne, *Montreuil Correspondence*, II, pp. 337–8.
4. Gardiner, *Constitutional Documents*, pp. 347–530.
5. Ashburnham, II, p. 121.
6. Gardiner, III, p. 317.
7. Abbott, I, pp. 575–8.
8. Sir James Turner, *Memoirs* (1839), p. 65.
9. Clarendon, IV, p. 390.
10. *Cit.* Gardiner, III, p. 480.
11. Ashburnham, II, p. 128.
12. British Library, Thomason Tracts 669, f. 13.333.
13. Charles I to the Prince of Wales from Newport, 25 November 1648, Clarendon, IV, pp. 454–5.
14. *Cit.* C.W. Firebrace, *Honest Harry* (1932), p. 163.
15. Sir Thomas Herbert's narrative, Stevenson, *op. cit.*, (1927), p. 161 *seq.*

13 The Trial and Execution of Charles I

1. *Old Parliamentary History*, xviii, pp. 226–8.
2. David Underdown, *Pride's Purge* (1971), p. 129.
3. *Ibid.*, p. 141.
4. Professor Underdown thinks this 'unlikely' (*ibid.*, p. 150), but after all Cromwell decided on the complete dissolution of the Rump of the Long Parliament in 1653, also under pressure from the Army.
5. C.V. Wedgwood, *The Trial of Charles I* (1964), p. 62.
6. Sir Thomas Herbert's narrative, Stevenson, *op. cit.*, pp. 174–5. Herbert calls Harrison a major, but he undoubtedly commanded a cavalry regiment in the New Model Army from 23 June 1647 onwards.
7. Underdown, *op. cit.*, ch. VIII.
8. I accept C.V. Wedgwood's views about Cromwell and Charles I's trial, not those of Gardiner and Underdown.
9. *The Trial and Execution of King Charles I* (1966) contains a facsimile of the account by Gilbert Mabbott which was the fullest official report of the trial. See also Roger Lockyer (ed.), *The Trial of Charles I* (1959), which reprints Mabbott's brief account. J.G. Muddiman, *Trial of Charles I* (1928), is unsatisfactory, but the texts and contents used in *State Trials* (1809), IV, pp. 990–1150 are extremely valuable.
10. *State Trials*, IV, p. 1102 *seq.* The death of Colonel William St George is recorded in Sir Henry Slingsby's diary.
11. Gardiner, III, p. 578.
12. Stevenson, *op. cit.*, p. 288.
13. *Eikon Basilike*, p. xxxiv, quoting Christopher Wordsworth, *Who Wrote Eikon Basilike?* (1824).

CONCLUSION

1. Richard Ollard, *The Image of the King* (1979), p. 39.
2. *Eikon Basilike*, p. 102.
3. Bruce, p. 80.
4. *Ibid.*, p. 98.
5. Russell, *The Causes of the English Civil War*, p. 191.
6. C.V. Wedgwood, *The King's Peace 1637–1641* (1955), pp. 70–3, 90–1.
7. *Letters of Queen Henriette Maria* (ed. M.A.E. Green 1857), pp. 63–4, *cit.* Russell, *The Causes of the English Civil War*, p. 204.
8. Clarendon, IV, p. 490.

9. Bruce, p. 20.
10. Charles to Nicholas from Huntingdon, 25 August 1645, *Correspondence of John Evelyn* (ed. Wheatley), IV, p. 170.
11. *Eikon Basilike*, p. 28.
12. Clarendon, IV, p. 489.
13. Russell, *The Causes of the English Civil War.*, p. 205.
14. Bruce, pp. 20–1, 81–2; *CSP (Dom)*, 1, p. 297.

APPENDIX A: The Strength of the Armies at Naseby

1. S.R. Gardiner, *History of the Great Civil War*, II, p. 208; J.H. Kenyon, *The Civil Wars in England* (1988), p. 142; H.C.B. Rogers, *Battles and Generals of the Civil Wars* (1968), p. 231.
2. *Transactions of the Lancashire and Cheshire Antiquarian Society*, LXVII (1957), p. 37.
3. Walker, p. 130.
4. Sprigge, p. 45; B. Whitelocke, *Memorials* (1853), I, p.448; Whitelocke, also wrote in his diary, which was published in 1990, p. 167; 'was the great battle of Naseby fought with great courage on both sides and was exceeding bloody. There was not 500 men odds of either Army'.
5. Peter Newman, *The Battle of Marston Moor 1644* (1981), pp. 5, 6, 43–4.
6. R. Symonds, *Diary* (1859), p. 182.
7. *John Evelyn Memoirs*, IV, p. 147.
8. *The Letter Books of Sir Samuel Luke* (ed. H.G. Tibbutt 1962), p. 297.
9. *Ibid.*, pp. 266, 310.
10. *Ibid.*, p. 319.
11. Barry Denton, *Naseby Fight* (1988), p. 54.
12. Young, p. 321.
13. Whitelocke, *op. cit.*, I, p. 452 states that Fiennes took 4,500 prisoners to London; another 500 were taken after Fiennes's convoy left (Thomason Tracts E 289 10). The figure of 5,000 is given both by Sprigge, p. 44, and in *A True Relation of Victory* (1645), Young, p. 373.
14. *Ibid.*, p. 337.
15. Gardiner, II, p. 259.
16. *Ibid.*, p. 584.

INDEX

Numbers in *italic* refer to illustrations.